These Forty Days

A Lenten Devotional

Jeren Rowell

𝘧

THE FOUNDRY
PUBLISHING

Copyright © 2015 by Jeren Rowell
The Foundry Publishing®
PO Box 419527
Kansas City, MO 64141
thefoundrypublishing.com

ISBN 978-0-8341-3512-3

Printed in the
United States of America

Cover Design: Sherman Schwartzrock
Interior Design: Sharon Page

10 9 8 7 6 5 4 3

Lord! Who throughout these forty days,
*   For us didst fast and pray,*
Teach us with Thee to mourn our sins,
*   And close by Thee to stay.*

As Thou with Satan didst contend,
*   And didst the victory win,*
Oh, give us strength in Thee to fight,
*   In Thee to conquer sin.*

As Thou didst hunger bear and thirst,
*   So teach us, gracious Lord,*
To die to self, and chiefly live
*   By Thy most holy Word.*

And through these days of penitence,
*   And through Thy Passiontide,*
Yea, evermore, in life and death,
*   Jesu! with us abide.*

Abide with us, that so, this life
*   Of suffering overpast,*
An Easter of unending joy
*   We may attain at last!*

—Claudia F. Hernaman,
"Lord, Who throughout These Forty Days" (1873)[1]

In memoriam
Judith Faith Bell Hooven (1956-99)
Judie worshipped God "in spirit and in truth" (John 4:24, KJV).

✳ Introduction to the Journey

These Forty Days is offered as a devotional companion for the season of Lent in the Christian year. The title refers not only to the forty days of the season from Ash Wednesday to Easter (not counting Sundays) but also to the wonderful nineteenth-century hymn of Claudia F. Hernaman, "Lord, Who throughout These Forty Days." The hymn has in view the desert temptation of our Lord as told in the Gospels. The story of the devil tempting Jesus is set within a period of fasting and prayer that is preparation for Jesus' public ministry and passion. It is notable throughout the Scriptures that times of desert preparation precede significant ministry. Besides Jesus' experience, we see it, for example, in the lives of Joseph, Moses, Elijah, Jonah, John the Baptist, and the apostle Paul. Christian people throughout the centuries have recognized the importance of special times for fasting and prayer. This is why the church very early on began to observe the season preceding Easter as an appropriate time for special spiritual focus. This was nothing new of course because Israel also observed special times for fasting and prayer, usually climaxing in feasts celebrating God's redemptive work among them (Passover, Pentecost, Ninth of Ab, Tabernacles, and Purim). Surely early Jewish Christians linked their long Passover tradition to the passion and death of Jesus, following the cues of the Teacher himself. This is simply to say that the rhythms of fasting and feasting, desert and oasis, discipline and joy, are not only well known to God's people but also seem to be essential components of spiritual growth.

One reason for this is that as the people of God we are a "storied" people. That is to say, the way that God has chosen to reveal himself to us is not so much through propositional truths and philosophies but largely in the telling of the story of our redemption. From creation to covenant to slavery to exodus to sacrificial worship to prophecy and judgment to silence to incarnation of God's self in Jesus of Nazareth to the pouring out of the Holy Spirit to the complete redemption of all things—what a story! This is why the Bible is so important to us because the Scriptures gather up these stories under the inspiration of the Spirit to continue shaping our identity as the people of God. Observing the seasons of the Christian year is simply part of remembering this story in a way that inspires, corrects, teaches, guides, and shapes us more and more into the likeness of Christ.

Those of us in the "believers' church" tradition have not connected as deeply to the rhythms of the Christian year (Advent, Christmas, Epiphany, Lent, Easter, Pentecost) as our brothers and sisters from more liturgical traditions. Sometimes people in our tradition worry that by observing Lent we are in danger of promoting dead ritual or form for its own sake. However, we, too, have understood something about the need for times of special spiritual focus. Revivals, camp meetings, assemblies, and prayer meetings have all been part of recognizing the importance of setting aside certain times for a deeper focus on what it means to follow the way of Jesus. And this is what the season of Lent is really about.

The word "lent" comes from a Latin word meaning "to lengthen" in the sense that the days are getting longer (in the northern hemisphere). Lent is popularly known as the time when Christians make a sacrifice of something in their lives. More importantly, Lent calls us away from easy religion. It presses upon our hearts the radical claims of the gospel. It confronts us with the obedience, suffering, and death of Jesus Christ, and it forces us to hear again his disturbing words, "If anyone would come after me, let him deny himself and take up his cross and follow me" (Mark 8:34).

So *These Forty Days* is offered as a simple guide for the reading of Scripture, reflection, prayer, and response. The primary emphasis is on the teaching of Jesus in what we have come to call the Sermon on the Mount, as presented to us in Matthew's gospel. The hope is that beginning the day with *intention* and *attention* will shape the remainder of the day toward a heightened sensitivity for how the Holy Spirit would like to teach us and guide us moment by moment. This is meant to be a friendly practice and not task driven. Embracing the discipline of this time is a good thing. Since Christian life is communal, we may even find it helpful to share this time with others—either at home or with one or two friends. However we want to approach it—alone or in the company of others—perhaps the most beneficial way to begin is by praying right now that God would make us hungry and thirsty to spend these first moments of the day with our minds tuned to the Father, Son, and Holy Spirit, who invite us into their life-giving fellowship.

May the Lord draw us closer during these days. May we come to Easter Day with a sense of prepared anticipation as we have never had before. And may the grace and peace of our Lord Jesus Christ be with us all.

* The Beginning of Lent
(Ash Wednesday to Day 4)

Ash Wednesday is a significant way to begin the season of Lent, since it links us back to where this story is headed: the triumphal entry of Jesus into Jerusalem and then his arrest, trial, suffering, and death. Traditionally the ashes of this day are obtained by burning the dried palm fronds that were used in the celebration of Palm Sunday the previous year. Typically the services of Ash Wednesday mark the beginning of the season of Lent through Scripture reading, songs of the season, and prayer. Many Christians begin a time of special fasting on Ash Wednesday that lasts throughout Lent (except Sundays). This can take many different forms, from giving up some particular food or habit to taking on a new spiritual discipline. Either way, the purpose is to move us to a deeper life of prayer.

In some places Ash Wednesday services include the opportunity to receive the imposition of ashes on the forehead during a service. This is a long tradition in the church that serves a couple of key purposes. One purpose is to remind us of the truth that life is short and we are utterly dependent upon God. The words spoken over us are, "For you are dust, and to dust you shall return." This comes from Genesis 3:19, where God spoke the consequences of sin over Adam and Eve. The ashes also serve as a sign to the world that we are among those who identify with Christ. In this way we bear witness throughout the day wherever we go that we are "crucified with Christ. It is no longer [we] who live, but Christ who lives in [us]" (Gal. 2:20).

❀ Ash Wednesday

BIBLE TEXT
Galatians 2:20

CONSIDER

This season of Lent raises for us the idea of *paschal* spirituality. This is an odd word and may be unfamiliar to us, but it has significance as we seek to begin this journey well. It comes from the Hebrew word *pesach*, which carries in part the meaning "from death to life." It has in mind the journey of Jesus, who became "obedient to the point of death, even death on a cross" (Phil. 2:8) and whom God raised from the dead. The death and resurrection of Jesus is the center of our faith. We live as disciples (followers) of Jesus with the mind-set of the apostle Paul when he said, "I die every day" (1 Cor. 15:31). The way of Jesus is marked by a daily death to sin, selfishness, and dishonesty—all that is contrary to Christ.

This is paschal spirituality, the way of Jesus. Author Brennan Manning discusses in his book *The Signature of Jesus* seven characteristics of this paschal spirituality that could guide us well during this Lenten season. The first characteristic is that paschal spirituality is *Christ centered*. This may seem obvious, but we must confess how often we are consumed with ourselves. The question that Jesus asked of Peter following the resurrection should pierce our hearts every day, "Do you love me more than these?" (John 21:15).

The second characteristic is that paschal spirituality is always *communal*. Our Christian faith is always personal but never private. During this Lenten journey we must ask ourselves, "What is my net influence on the community of faith?"

The third characteristic of paschal spirituality is that it *believes in redemption*. Christians should be optimistic people. We have not given up on the world, because we know that God is at work in the world by the Holy Spirit to redeem the world and everything in it.

The fourth characteristic of paschal spirituality is that we consider ourselves to be *crucified with Christ*. We respond to God's forgiveness with a life fully surrendered to God. As Christians we no longer work to protect our personal rights, but now we fulfill our responsibilities, our service to Christ.

The fifth characteristic of paschal spirituality is that it is *joyful and optimistic*. Our life in Christ is anchored in hope and always looks forward. We ought to attract people to our faith quite literally by the fun there is in being a Christian.

The sixth characteristic is that paschal spirituality *promotes unity without uniformity*. Mature Christian faith appreciates the rich variety of personalities who make up the church.

Finally, the seventh characteristic is that paschal spirituality *regards persons as free*. Therefore, we stop trying to control and manipulate each other. This may be the hardest lesson of all, for sometimes we try to secure our own faith by forcing others to look just like us.

READING

Death and resurrection are not one-time events that occur only at the end of our journey. They are the pattern of our lives day after day.[1] "Each time we let go of the past to embrace the future we relive the paschal journey of Jesus in our flesh. Each time we allow our fears or selfishness to die, we break through to new life. Each time we open ourselves to the Spirit so that he can break down the walls of suspicion and bitterness, we come home to ourselves, the community, and the Lord."[2]

—*Brennan Manning and John Heagle*

PRAYER

Father, as we begin this Lenten journey, we pray your watchful care over us as we seek to overcome evil by the power and grace of the Spirit. Through our sacrifices of self, make us more like Jesus, in whose name we pray. Amen.

DISCIPLINE (RESPONSE)

Think prayerfully through each of the seven characteristics of the paschal journey. To what degree are these marks of the way of Jesus evident in your life?

BLESSING

Go now into this holy day in the power of the Holy Spirit to bear witness to the Savior who gave himself for us. And may the peace of Christ be with you.

❂ Thursday (after Ash Wednesday)

BIBLE TEXT

Joel 2:12-17

CONSIDER

The church wisely assigns this reading from the prophet Joel at the beginning of our Lenten journey. The connection is evident as we hear the exhortation to "consecrate a fast" (v. 15). Hopefully you have already begun some discipline of fasting and prayer. The purpose is to draw closer to the Lord. This is very good. However, if it goes no further than our personal discipline, it remains something less than full-bodied discipleship. Could it be that our observance of Lenten discipline has become far too individual? We tend to ask questions such as, "How will *I* hear from God afresh this season? What should *I* give up during this time of fasting?" Joel's call to repentance and fasting is a call to the entire community. No one is dismissed, because what happens during these times is so important, so life shaping. So the preacher says, "Assemble the elders; gather the children, even nursing infants" (v. 16).

This is no incidental detail in the call to God's people. The intergenerational nature of the community of faith is essential to faithful worship and witness. What if a rich experience of Lenten renewal awaits those congregations that will call the community of faith back together? Perhaps this is a good time to rethink the inclusion of children in the gatherings of the church for worship. What would the Lord say to us during this Lenten journey about the care and intention we are giving to discipling our children? This is not to focus exclusively on the nuclear family. Life in the community of faith calls us beyond responsibility for our own household. Are there children or teenagers in your congregation or in your neighborhood that need the influence of a godly mentor?

The prophet seems to be saying to God's people that the nearness of the day of the Lord calls for us to repent of our individualized, privatized ways of living and turn back toward not only the Lord but also toward one another.

READING

The prophet Joel responds to a devastating plague of locusts that has come upon the nation and attributes this event to the judgment of God (Joel 1). In Joel 2:1-11, he likens the onslaught of insects to an invading army and thus evokes the impending Day of the Lord with all its fierce judgment. Joel calls for the people to respond with a collective fast and a season of repentance. "Return to me with all your heart," God says. Do you see anything befalling our nation or global community that should impel us to collective humility and repentance?

—*Bobby Gross*[3]

PRAYER

Lord, we know that you are not impressed by our ability but call us to humility. Save us from the enticements of this world that would blur our clear focus upon you. Fix our gaze upon your beauty and holiness that we would come to desire nothing but you. In the name of Jesus our Savior we pray. Amen.

DISCIPLINE (RESPONSE)

As we respond to the Lord's call through Joel to "gather the people" (v. 16), how might this be expressed in your household? How might this be expressed in your community of faith? How might this be expressed in your neighborhood? Is there a greater intentionality of gathering that should mark our communities during these special days of fasting and prayer?

BLESSING

As you go forth into this new day, may your life become a source of blessing to all around. May the people you encounter today be drawn closer to God because of your love. May your Christlike character shine through every conversation of this day. And may the peace of Christ be with you.

❁ Friday (after Ash Wednesday)

BIBLE TEXT
Isaiah 58:1-7

CONSIDER

Fasting for its own sake is not what God desires from us. The people of God to whom Isaiah is preaching were seriously engaged in fasting. Evidently they thought that God was somehow obligated to intervene on their behalf as an appropriate response to their spiritual discipline. They are disappointed, however, that God is not responding to their fasting as they hoped. Why not? Fasting without true repentance is just fasting. It misses the point. Fasting for its own sake has some value, but it does not of its own accord accomplish what God means to accomplish in us through times of spiritual discipline.

Isaiah preaches a message to help the people recognize that in order for fasting to be efficacious it must move us to repentance. In other words, our acts of piety are not our holiness. Our acts of piety are instruments that, by the grace of God, do the work of aligning our heart, mind, soul, and body to the values, priorities, and activities of the kingdom of God.

So Isaiah calls his people to bear the fruit of repentance by allowing God to so change their thinking and feeling that it moves them from religious practices to practical ministry. And these ministries, just like fasting, are not for their own sake. By the power of the Spirit they become a sign of God's redemptive, healing, and restoring work in the world. These are the works of justice, compassion, and healing.

As we move through these days of Lent, hopefully we will grow through embracing specific spiritual disciplines, including fasting. But more important than achieving "success" in our discipline is allowing the Spirit to change our minds about how we are living. Perhaps God wants to rearrange the values and priorities of our lives to align us with the kingdom of God. The point of Lent is not to feel sorrowful for our sin and brokenness. The point of Lent is to come under the transforming grace of God in a way that changes our lives. Holiness means we are set apart for God's holy purposes. The pressing question of Lent is, "To what degree is my life truly set apart for God and God's mission in this world?"

READING

A fast is a day to afflict the soul; if it does not express true sorrow for sin, and does not promote the putting away of sin, it is not a fast. . . . To be liberal and merciful is more acceptable to God than mere fasting, which, without them, is vain and hypocritical. Many who seem humble in God's house, are hard at home, and harass their families. But no man's faith justifies, which does not work by love. Yet persons, families, neighbourhoods, churches, or nations, show repentance and sorrow for sin, by keeping a fast sincerely, and, from right motives, repenting, and doing good works. The heavy yoke of sin and oppression must be removed. As sin and sorrow dry the bones and weaken the strongest human constitution; so the duties of kindness and charity strengthen and refresh both body and mind.

—*Matthew Henry*[4]

PRAYER

I need Thee to teach me day by day, according to each day's opportunities and needs. Give me, O my Lord, that purity of conscience which alone can receive, which alone can improve Thy inspirations. My ears are dull, so that I cannot hear Thy voice. My eyes are dim, so that I cannot see Thy tokens. Thou alone canst quicken my hearing, and purge my sight, and cleanse and renew my heart. Teach me to sit at Thy feet, and to hear Thy word—Amen. Amen.[5]

DISCIPLINE (RESPONSE)

As you walk through the routine of this day, invite the Lord to speak to you about every movement, every expenditure, and every activity of this day. Ask, "Lord, is this pleasing to you? Is this how you would have me to use the gifts that you have given to me?" What would the Spirit teach you today about a life of true fasting that involves loving acts of compassion and justice?

BLESSING

May God the Holy Spirit enliven your awareness today so that every conversation, decision, and activity is offered to the Lord as your worship. And may the worship of your whole life rise before God as a beautiful offering. The peace of Christ be with you.

✹ Saturday (after Ash Wednesday)

BIBLE TEXT

Psalm 51:1-12

CONSIDER

These are the words of a guilty man. We know these words; they strike a chord with us. They are familiar words because all of us have been here in one way or another. The particulars of our guilt may be different, but we can readily identify with the feelings. When we feel guilty, we think that everyone probably knows about our sin, that everyone we meet can probably peer right into our very soul and see the awful thing we have done.

David was suffering with guilt. This psalm is ascribed to him out of the aftermath of his affair with Bathsheba. David tried to go on with life until a preacher named Nathan skillfully confronted David and helped him to tell the truth. When David was faced with the truth of his sin, he was struck with a kind of guilt that could cause him to tear his clothes and put ashes over his head. This was a guilt that could make him say, "My bones wasted away through my groaning all day long. For day and night your hand was heavy upon me; my strength was dried up as by the heat of summer" (Ps. 32:3-4).

What is our best response when we find ourselves suffering under a load of guilt? First, we need to be clear about whether or not this is true guilt that rightfully belongs to us or false guilt that some of us easily load upon ourselves for other reasons. A conversation with a pastor or mature Christian friend may be the first step. True guilt is when we clearly know that we have sinned. When this is our situation, confession is the only way forward. We must tell the truth, to ourselves, to God, and perhaps to someone else. The good news is that we are not left to ourselves in this confession. Through the grace of our Lord Jesus there is forgiveness and the cleansing of our hearts that David describes in the poignant words of Psalm 51. Through that cleansing, the joy of the Lord can indeed be restored.

READING

The confession of sin is based on the grace of God. "Be gracious" . . . is the first word of the psalm. The plea appeals to God's steadfast love and abundant mercy (v. 1). The prayer is not merely an expression of human remorse . . . ; it looks beyond self to God and lays hold on the marvelous possibilities of God's grace. Confession of sin is already on the way to justification because it is first of all a response to grace. It is the act in which we humans acknowledge what we are before God and what God is for us. We are sinners; God is gracious.

—James L. Mays[6]

PRAYER

Almighty God, to you all hearts are open, all desires known, and from you no secrets are hid: Cleanse the thoughts of our hearts by the inspiration of your Holy Spirit, that we may perfectly love you, and worthily magnify your holy Name; through Christ our Lord. Amen.[7]

DISCIPLINE (RESPONSE)

Our noisy world conspires with the enemy of our souls to keep us from hearing our own conscience and the "gentle whisper" (1 Kings 19:12, NIV) of the Spirit. Would you dare on this Saturday to find a space to become silent before God for a sustained period? Invite the Holy Spirit to speak to you and to show you any unconfessed sin. Do not be afraid. The God who convicts of sin (John 16:8) is also the Lord who creates a clean heart (Ps. 51:10).

BLESSING

May the Lord grant you courage to tell the truth about yourself. May the Holy Spirit guide you into all truth and grant you grace to confess your need completely. And may you know the joy of sin forgiven and of a heart cleansed by faith. By the mercies of God may you know the peace of Christ in all its fullness.

✳ The Second Week of Lent
(First Sunday to Day 10)

With the first Sunday in Lent we move into the first full week of the season. Now we move to the body of Scripture commonly known as the Sermon on the Mount. We will focus on the version by Matthew, who gives us this sustained teaching of Jesus in chapters 5 through 7 of his gospel.

❀ First Sunday in Lent

(Note: the formal designation of Sunday in the season of Lent is "Sunday *in* Lent" rather than "Sunday *of* Lent." This is because Sunday is not a fast day but the Lord's Day, when we celebrate the resurrection.)

BIBLE TEXT

Matthew 5:1-12

CONSIDER

The opening lines of the Sermon on the Mount are often called the Beatitudes. They portray the attitudes of being in a right relationship with God. These words remind us that being Christian is not first about *doing* right things but about *being* the right person—one with a right attitude. These beatitudes are words of blessing. Some translate the Greek word behind "blessed" as "happy" or "privileged." It could even be rendered "congratulations." It is a word about a blessing from God, a special grace given. Yet as we hear these beatitudes, it can be hard to imagine how some of the things described in them and the concept of blessing go together. Jesus speaks of being poor, grieving, being meek and persecuted. He then has the audacity to say, "Congratulations to you when this is your condition." It doesn't make sense. Perhaps what Jesus would like us to see as he begins to talk about the basics of discipleship is that having the right kind of attitude goes a lot deeper than having the right circumstances.

What Jesus is talking about here in such a beautiful and poetic way is a manner of living where we take our cues not primarily from the world around us but from a focus on him that enables us to approach life differently from what would otherwise be the case. For example, Jesus says the attitude of a Christian is not prideful self-righteousness but mourning. We are to face our sinfulness and admit that it has hurt God and others and repent of it. Only then can we know God's comfort and peace as he forgives and cleanses us. People who live in this way do not become judgmental. They have mercy and compassion and can offer forgiveness to those who hurt them because they remember how much they have been forgiven. The Christian way of living is to be a person of meekness, which does not mean being weak. It means open, teachable, not defensive, gentle, and under control.

Do you get the idea? Jesus is saying that if you really want to be Christian, if you really want to walk the way of Jesus, then your core attitudes will be different from what you see in the world. Here is the good news: this does not depend on your strength or your ability to choose the right attitude. God is able to change your mind and give you the blessing of attitudes that reflect the very character of Jesus.

READING

If Jesus is a Teacher only, then all He can do is to tantalise us by erecting a standard we cannot come anywhere near. But if by being born again from above, we know Him first as Saviour, we know that He did not come to teach us only: *He came to make us what He teaches we should be.* The Sermon on the Mount is a statement of the life we will live when the Holy Spirit is having His way with us.

—*Oswald Chambers*[1]

PRAYER

Heavenly Father, may your loving pursuit of this wandering child draw me more and more into the warmth of your love. Deliver me from the thorns around that threaten to choke out the life you have given me. Fill me with your Spirit that I might honor you moment by moment of this new day. Walk with me, Jesus. I need you. Amen.

DISCIPLINE (RESPONSE)

As you walk through this day, invite the Holy Spirit to correct you at any time that your attitude begins to reflect the values and priorities of this world rather than life in the kingdom of God. And if you dare, invite someone close to you to help you with this discipline.

BLESSING

May the joy of the Lord be your strength throughout this Lord's Day. May your worship rise from a grateful heart. Go into this day to love and serve as Jesus would do. And may the peace of Christ be with you.

❋ Monday in the Second Week of Lent

BIBLE TEXT

Matthew 5:3

CONSIDER

"Blessed" is a wonderful word. Everyone wants to be blessed. The idea of blessing is central in the story of God's people. It's especially poignant in the desperate cry of Esau in Genesis 27 when he realized that with his impulsive decision he squandered his father's blessing. Esau cries, "Bless me, even me also, O my father" (v. 38). All of us need blessing. We long for it, hope for it, and languish when we do not receive it. So when we hear Jesus begin with a word of blessing, we are hopeful. This should be good. The problem is that what comes after the promise of blessing is not what we would expect. We hear words such as "poor," "mourn," "meek," "hungry," and "persecuted." These don't sound much like blessing.

What Jesus seems to be suggesting is that an authentic poverty of spirit can be a blessed way of living. "For Matthew, the *poor in spirit* are those who find themselves waiting, empty-handed, upon God alone for their hope and deliverance."[2] Waiting with empty-handed dependency is right at the center of an appropriate Lenten posture. The world teaches us to be self-sufficient and accomplished, needing nothing or no one. This is not the way of the kingdom of heaven, nor is it the attitude of a follower of Jesus.

Do we live each day in the awareness that without God we are lost and without hope? Do we recognize that every day, every breath, is a gift of grace? Do we daily confess that we are not capable of providing a blessed life for ourselves or our loved ones? These recognitions move us in the direction of the poverty of spirit that finds blessing in the kingdom of God.

Hilke Shultz was a dear saint who lived in a tenement apartment on the south side of Chicago. It was my blessing for several years to visit her there regularly. She was poor by every measure of the world. Each time I visited her, I began our conversation with, "Hello, Sister Shultz. How are you today?" Her response was consistent and authentic: "I'm blessed; I'm blessed; I'm blessed." Was she ignoring the facts? No, she had simply surrendered the world's way of reading blessing to the values of the kingdom of heaven. And in that regard she was *blessed* indeed.

READING

As long as we have a conceited, self-righteous idea that we can do the thing if God will help us, God has to allow us to go on until we break the neck of our ignorance over some obstacle, then we will be willing to come and receive from Him. The bedrock of Jesus Christ's Kingdom is poverty, not possession; not decisions for Jesus Christ, but a sense of absolute futility, "I cannot begin to do it." Then, says Jesus, "Blessed are you." That is the entrance, and it takes us a long while to believe we are poor. The knowledge of our own poverty brings us to the moral frontier where Jesus Christ works.

—*Oswald Chambers*[3]

PRAYER

But may all who seek you
   rejoice and be glad in you;
may those who love your salvation
   say continually, "Great is the LORD!"
As for me, I am poor and needy,
   but the Lord takes thought for me.
You are my help and my deliverer;
   do not delay, O my God! (Ps. 40:16-17)

DISCIPLINE (RESPONSE)

Are you willing to wait on God to supply your need? Where are you tempted to take matters into your own hands to secure your future? Would there be an act of trust and discipline for you today that would move you from trusting your own ability toward truly trusting in God? It may be an act of sacrificial giving. It may be the refusal to accept indebtedness. It may be as simple as releasing your worry about tomorrow to God, who promises to take care of you.

BLESSING

May the Lord grant you courage to embrace the poverty of spirit that makes us truly open to God's blessing. May the Lord help you to unmask the lies of this world. And may the Lord help you to resist temptations to make your own way. The peace of Christ be with you.

❋ Tuesday in the Second Week of Lent

BIBLE TEXT

Matthew 5:4

CONSIDER

Our first read of this beatitude may cause us to think of times when we have personally experienced loss. Some of us know mourning at a depth that others of us only wonder about. Our world is generally uncomfortable with mourning. Some cultures know how to embrace times of grief and allow long periods of mourning. Contemporary Western cultures seem set on controlling grief. Dead bodies are whisked away quickly to be dealt with by professionals. Jesus is unafraid to acknowledge that life in this broken world will shower us with opportunities to mourn, but this is not the end of it. Jesus says "Blessed are those who mourn," not because of the mourning, but because in the midst of grief is where the beautiful comfort of God can be known.

Roger Hahn points out that the promise of comfort in this beatitude is expressed in the passive voice, "shall be comforted."[4] It is a construction that is used often in the New Testament to suggest God without speaking the divine name. Clearly the source of our comfort is God himself by the ministry of the Comforter, the Holy Spirit. In other words, this is grace carried by our hope in the risen Lord Jesus Christ, who conquered death and the grave.

There is another sense of mourning that may be in view here. It is hinted by Matthew's evident echoing of the language of Isaiah 61, which remarkably parallels much of these beatitudes. There, the mourning is because of sin and God's judgment. However, even when we find ourselves under the discipline of God, the promise of comfort comes to God's people: "to give them a beautiful headdress instead of ashes, the oil of gladness instead of mourning, the garment of praise instead of a faint spirit" (v. 3). Perhaps part of the gift of mourning includes the chance to repent from self-righteous pride and remember that we are sinners deserving God's judgment and in need of God's grace. The self-righteous person has nothing to mourn. Jesus invites us to face our sinfulness, admit that it has hurt God and others, and repent. Only then can we know God's comfort and peace as he forgives and cleanses us.

READING

These troubles and distresses that you go through in these waters are no sign that God hath forsaken you; but are sent to try you, whether you will call to mind that which heretofore you have received of his goodness, and live upon him in your distresses.

Then I saw in my dream, that Christian was in a muse a while. To whom also Hopeful added these words, Be of good cheer, Jesus Christ maketh thee whole. And with that Christian brake out with a loud voice, Oh, I see him again; and he tells me, "When thou passest through the waters, I will be with thee." . . . Then they both took courage, and the enemy was after that as still as a stone, until they were gone over. Christian, therefore, presently found ground to stand upon, and so it followed that the rest of the river was but shallow. Thus they got over.

—*John Bunyan*[5]

PRAYER

O God, the protector of all who trust in you, without whom nothing is strong, nothing is holy: Increase and multiply upon us your mercy; that, with you as our ruler and guide, we may so pass through things temporal, that we lose not the things eternal; through Jesus Christ our Lord, who lives and reigns with you and the Holy Spirit, one God, for ever and ever. Amen.[6]

DISCIPLINE (RESPONSE)

Does there remain a grief in your soul that too often settles like a dark cloud over the day? In addition to offering this grief to God anew, would you consider taking the risk one more time to speak it aloud to a trusted friend? Breaking the silence may, by God's grace, become part of opening the gift of God's comfort.

BLESSING

"Blessed be the God and Father of our Lord Jesus Christ, the Father of mercies and God of all comfort, who comforts us in all our affliction, so that we may be able to comfort those who are in any affliction, with the comfort with which we ourselves are comforted by God" (2 Cor. 1:3-4). The peace of Christ be with you.

❂ Wednesday in the Second Week of Lent

BIBLE TEXT

Matthew 5:5

CONSIDER

These beatitudes stand in contrast to the self-righteousness and pride that can so easily overtake us. The Christian way of living according to Jesus is to be a person of meekness, which has nothing to do with weakness. The term connotes "an attitude rather than a condition."[7] It means "open," "teachable," "not defensive," "gentle," and "under control." It sounds something like Paul's description of the fruit of the Spirit in Galatians 5:22-23, which is contrasted there with the opposite of meekness: "enmity, strife, jealousy, fits of anger, rivalries, dissensions, divisions, envy," and so on (vv. 20-21). Meekness has the strength to give a gentle answer that "turns away wrath" (Prov. 15:1). It is strong enough and secure enough that it does need to answer every accusation or return hurtful words for a hurtful word received. This beatitude echoes the language of Psalm 37, which encourages us not to worry about protecting ourselves in the face of those who choose violence. The psalmist says, "The meek shall inherit the land and delight themselves in abundant peace" (v. 11). This psalm goes on to give us lots of practical advice about how to stand secure in the midst of a world bent on wickedness. And then there is this promise, "The LORD knows the days of the blameless, and their heritage will remain forever; they are not put to shame in evil times" (vv. 18-19).

A great temptation in our time is to think that our future can be secured through our own efforts or through the efforts of societies or governments. The Bible never promises this. Rather, our security is found in trusting God so completely that we know true peace and rest even in the midst of threats all around. This is what the Hebrews meant by *shalom*. It means "wholeness" that is only whole because it is given by God. It means "completeness" because of God's loving-kindness (*chesed*). It means "fullness" that is due to God's great grace. The meek are those who are learning that God alone is their Source; therefore, they do not seek to secure their own way but trust in the God who is "making all things new" (Rev. 21:5).

READING

The gentleness of Jesus with sinners flowed from his ability to read their hearts and to detect the sincerity and goodness there. Behind men's grumpiest poses and most puzzling defense mechanisms, behind their arrogance and airs, behind their silence, sneers and curses, Jesus saw little children who hadn't been loved enough and who had ceased growing because someone had ceased believing in them. His extraordinary sensitivity and compassion caused Jesus (and later the apostles) to speak of the faithful as children, no matter how tall, rich, clever, and successful they might be.

—*Brennan Manning*[8]

PRAYER

Give me Thy grace, good Lord, to set the world at naught; to set my mind fast upon Thee; and not to hang upon the blast of men's mouths.

To be content to be solitary; not to long for worldly company; little and little utterly to cast off the world, and rid my mind of all the business thereof. . . .

. . . to walk the narrow way that leadeth to life.[9] Amen.

DISCIPLINE (RESPONSE)

Is there evidence that your manner of living pushes others away rather than draws them near? Do people confide in you? Does anyone come to you seeking wisdom? A life of Christlike meekness is a gift of grace, but it also develops in the disciplines of James 1:19: "Let every person be quick to hear, slow to speak, slow to anger." Does your life reflect this wisdom?

BLESSING

Go into this day in the power of the Spirit and with the confidence to live in the strength of meekness. "Do not be conformed to this world" (Rom. 12:2). May the Lord assist you to trade the anxieties of this world for the peace of the kingdom of God. The grace and peace of our Lord Jesus be with you.

✸ Thursday in the Second Week of Lent

BIBLE TEXT
Matthew 5:6

CONSIDER

Have you ever been really hungry? We say it often, "I'm hungry. When are we going to eat?" or "Mom, what's for dinner? I'm about to starve to death." We say it often, but have you ever really been hungry? There certainly are times when we may think we are hungry. There may even be a few times when our bodies have acted strangely with shakes or sweats after not eating for an extended period. Some would say this is not really hunger but the temper tantrums of spoiled stomachs. Truthfully, this is the only hunger many of us have experienced. There are in fact many people in our world who experience true hunger. In the time it takes to write this paragraph someone somewhere in the world has closed his or her eyes and died of hunger.

For most of us to ask the question "Are you hungry?" seems a silly question. So how could we ever really identify with Jesus' words: "Blessed are those who hunger . . . for they shall be satisfied"? We begin here because our physical lives are so often an expression of what is happening in our spiritual lives. Our hunger for bread is at its best a reflection of much deeper hungers. We hunger not only for bread but also for the other gifts that sustain life: love, meaning, direction, purpose, and hope.

Clearly Jesus cared deeply about our physical needs. In Luke's gospel a similar saying seems more focused on physical hunger that will be satisfied in the kingdom of God. Here, in Matthew, Jesus' words are expanded to include "hunger and thirst *for righteousness*." What is the righteousness for which we should hunger and thirst? It is the righteousness of living an upright life, and it is also the righteousness of God's gift to us. The gospel message is that a holy God not only requires our holiness but also provides our holiness through the gift of the Holy Spirit.

The hunger and thirst of which Jesus speaks is not something we must manufacture. This passionate desire for God is a gift of grace. However, we do have the ability either to dampen our hearts toward the work of the Spirit or to nurture our hearts in that direction. This is the purpose of spiritual discipline. The beautiful promise of Jesus is that our hunger and thirst "shall be satisfied." In John's gospel Jesus said it like this: "I am the bread of life; whoever comes to me shall not hunger, and whoever believes in me shall never thirst" (6:35).

READING

It is possible either to sustain and strengthen this burning of the spirit, or to quench it. It is warmed above all by acts of love towards God and our neighbor—this, indeed, is the essence of the spiritual life—by a general fidelity to all God's commandments, with a quiet conscience, by deeds that are pitiless to our own soul and body, and by prayer and thoughts of God. The spirit is quenched by distraction of the attention from God and God's works, by excessive anxiety about worldly matters, by indulgence in sensual pleasure, by pandering to carnal desires, and by infatuation with material things. If this spirit is quenched, then the Christian life will be quenched too.

—The Art of Prayer[10]

PRAYER

Lord, by the abiding presence of your Spirit, grant us the power to resist temptation and to overcome sin. Make us discerning and wise as we walk in a world so often given over to selfish desire. Grant us the joy of full obedience, in the name of Jesus Christ our Savior. Amen.

DISCIPLINE (RESPONSE)

Fasting from food for spiritual purposes has a long tradition. Undoubtedly this is because food is so essential to our existence. Yet food can also become an idol, something that controls our lives rather than serves its intended function. In order to put food in its place, would you consider fasting a meal today or perhaps fasting for a full day this week? Let the Spirit guide you in what you should do. Most of all, search your heart to see if there is within it a genuine hunger and thirst for righteousness.

BLESSING

As you walk through this day, may the demanding voices of your physical desires give way to the voice of the Spirit, calling you to hunger and thirst for righteousness. May the grace of God draw you deeper into the wellspring of living water and to the very Bread of Life. And may the peace of Christ be with you.

✸ Friday in the Second Week of Lent

BIBLE TEXT
Matthew 5:7

CONSIDER

Later in Matthew's gospel we will encounter the story of the unmerciful servant (18:21-35). The idea of the story is basic. When a person has been the recipient of mercy, it is expected that such a person would now extend the same to others. However, in contrast to what is expected, the story, as Jesus tells it, shocks the senses. That a servant who was forgiven so great a debt could so quickly be unwilling to release another from a much smaller debt is astounding. The master in the story expresses the incredulity: "And should not you have had mercy on your fellow servant, as I had mercy on you?" (v. 33).

The Bible speaks clearly that all of us are recipients of God's mercy. Paul writes, "You were at one time disobedient to God but now have received mercy" (Rom. 11:30). Peter says, "Blessed be the God and Father of our Lord Jesus Christ! According to his great mercy, he has caused us to be born again to a living hope through the resurrection of Jesus Christ from the dead" (1 Pet. 1:3). This is the reality from which we now have the capacity to be merciful toward others. That is, we are merciful in direct response to the pardon we have received from God when we deserved nothing but death.

This beatitude, like the other beatitudes, is not an exhortation. It is not a command to be merciful. This is a proverb—an observation of how life works under the reign of God. It simply makes sense that when one has been the recipient of a great mercy, one would purposefully, in grateful response, live as a person of mercy. This is easily said and perhaps easily recognized in principle but not so easily done. What could keep us from offering the mercy that we ourselves have received?

Any number of things could mute our mercy, but chief among the possibilities would likely be a failure to recognize just how much we have been forgiven. This is part of why a purposeful Lenten journey is important to our spiritual growth. During these days we should especially be remembering the depth of our sin that took our Lord Jesus to

30

the cross. This is not for the purpose of wallowing in our guilt but of avoiding spiritual pride by daily surrendering our righteousness, which is nothing more than filthy rags, to the righteousness of Christ, in which we are clothed by grace.

READING

[The merciful] have an irresistible love for the down-trodden, the sick, the wretched, the wronged, the outcast and all who are tortured with anxiety. They go out and seek all who are enmeshed in the toils of sin and guilt. No distress is too great, no sin too appalling for their pity. If any man falls into disgrace, the merciful will sacrifice their own honour to shield him and take his shame upon themselves. They will be found consorting with publicans and sinners, careless of the shame they incur thereby. In order that they may be merciful, they cast away the most priceless treasure of human life, their personal dignity and honour. For the only honour and dignity they know is their Lord's own mercy, to which alone they owe their very lives.

—*Dietrich Bonhoeffer*[11]

PRAYER

Father, hallowed be your name.
Your kingdom come.
Give us each day our daily bread,
and forgive us our sins,
   for we ourselves forgive everyone who is indebted to us.
And lead us not into temptation. (Luke 11:2-4)

DISCIPLINE (RESPONSE)

As you open your heart to the Lord at the beginning of this day, would the Spirit bring to mind anyone who needs your mercy? Is there perhaps someone from whom you have withheld your mercy? As one who has received mercy, is there someone to whom you may now be merciful in the name of Jesus Christ, who forgives you?

BLESSING

Go into this day by the power of the Spirit to bear witness to the love and grace of Jesus Christ. May God grant you courage today to extend mercy as you have been shown mercy. And may mercy return to you as a gift of grace. The peace of Christ be with you.

❁ Saturday in the Second Week of Lent

BIBLE TEXT
Matthew 5:8

CONSIDER

This beatitude seems to carry echoes of Psalm 24, where the writer asks the key question of all who would seek the presence of God: "Who shall ascend the hill of the LORD? And who shall stand in his holy place?" (v. 3). The simple yet profound answer comes: "He who has clean hands and a pure heart" (v. 4). Upon hearing the requirement we may quickly assume that we are disqualified. It is easy for us to hear this as a requirement for flawless behavior. However, the idea of a pure heart is centered on our will or the motive behind our behaviors. This is not to suggest that actions or behaviors are inconsequential. Jesus makes clear that what defiles a person is not what goes in from the outside but what emerges from deep within the human heart (Mark 7:14-23). In other words, there is a causative connection between the heart and the actions of a person. What this beatitude calls for is true correspondence between one's actions and one's motives.

This may not seem a particularly difficult posture to attain. Most of us no doubt consider ourselves to be among the pure in heart. The challenge is that we are living in the midst of a world where duplicity is not only common but encouraged. We are taught to put our best foot forward. This can easily carry into our spiritual lives as we learn to present ourselves outwardly in ways that mask our true spiritual condition. This is why the community of faith is so critical to our spiritual development. Some people these days are asserting that they can follow Christ without having to bother with the church. This is an unbiblical view. Eugene Peterson writes, "If we are serious about growing up in Christ, we have to deal with church."[12] At the heart of serious discipleship is the kind of fierce accountability that flows from Paul's understanding of what it means to be on this "Way" together. He writes to the Ephesian Christians, "Submit to one another out of reverence for Christ" (Eph. 5:21, NIV). Purity of heart cannot be known in isolation. It is only developed and experienced in *koinōnia* (Gk., "fellowship").

32

READING

We often hear the criticism that the Church is afflicted with piety, but the real trouble is that its piety is not deep enough! Since the materials are available, all that is needed is the recognition of where they are, and the will to employ them. An important contribution would be the liberation of the term "piety" from its present damaging connotations, reinstating it as a term of respect. We, indeed, still have a little piety; we say a few hasty prayers; we sing meaningfully a few hymns; we read snatches from the Bible. But all of this is far removed from the massive dose that we sorely need if we are to be the men and women who can perform a healing service in our generation.

—Elton Trueblood[13]

PRAYER

Hear our prayers, O Lord, and consider our desires. Give unto us true humility, a meek and quiet spirit, a loving and a friendly, a holy and a useful, manner of life; bearing the burdens of our neighbors, denying ourselves, and studying to benefit others, and to please Thee in all things. Grant us to be righteous in performing promises, loving to our relatives, careful of our charges; to be gentle and easy to be entreated, slow to anger, and readily prepared for every good work—Amen.[14]

DISCIPLINE (RESPONSE)

As you inventory the key relationships of your life, are you enjoying the gift of authentic accountability? Do you pray with and for others, that we would use fully the grace of God to make us pure in heart? If you do not have this kind of relationship in your life, would you pray today that God would show you whom to approach and invite to consider this kind of spiritual accountability?

BLESSING

As you walk into a new day, may it be with a heightened awareness that the Lord goes with you, helping you to live from a pure heart. May every thought, every word, and every action of this day be fully surrendered to Christ. And may the quality of your life inspire others to walk the way of Jesus. The peace of Christ be with you.

* The Third Week of Lent

(Second Sunday to Day 16)

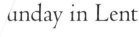

unday in Lent

-12

The seventh and eighth beatitudes are considered together today. Peacemaking and persecution are neighbors. This is the case not only because peacemakers are unafraid to march headlong into places of discord and strife but also because the manner and work of peacemakers is not always appreciated. Sometimes those who are for peace find themselves the target of persecution.

It is important to note that the promised blessing is not for those who *enjoy* peace. Most people would prefer peace. This blessing is for peace*makers*. It is for those who work to bring wholeness, healing, and reconciliation into the fractured relationships of this world. Peacemakers are people who have learned to bring both grace and truth together in the way that Jesus modeled it. John's gospel introduces Jesus to us in this way: he was "full of grace and truth" (John 1:14). Most of us tend toward one side or the other: we either tend to be grace givers or tend to be truth tellers. The way of Jesus is to live in the balance of these essential postures, and when we do, we are able to become peacemakers. Peacemakers do not simply smooth things over; they tell the truth with love. Peacemakers do not manipulate others with facts; they listen until the shouting stops and people begin actually to talk to one another. Peacemaking is at the core of reflecting the character of Jesus. No wonder he says that when we give ourselves to peacemaking, we are considered "children of God" (Matt. 5:9, NIV).

The problem with this kind of proactive peacemaking, in contrast to passive nonresistance, is that it often attracts the fury of those who prefer conflict or prefer to demand their own way. Persecution can come our way because of righteousness. That is, our work of announcing the universal reign of God in Christ will bring us into conflict with those who are living by other agendas. We should not be surprised at this but should instead "rejoice" (v. 12). We do not rejoice because of the persecution itself but because suffering persecution for the sake of righteousness puts us right in line with the purposes of God in this world as expressed through the prophets before us. In other words, being persecuted for our peacemaking work is an indication that our lives (individually and together) have become a sign of the in-breaking kingdom of God.

READING

Is it possible to carry out the Beatitudes? Never! Unless God can do what Jesus Christ says He can, unless He can give us the Holy Spirit who will remake us and bear us into a new realm. The essential element of the life of a saint is simplicity, and Jesus Christ makes the motive of godliness gloriously simple, viz.: Be carefully careless about everything saving your relationship to Me. The motive of a disciple is to be well-pleasing to God. The true blessedness of the saint is in determinedly making and keeping God first. Herein lies the disproportion between Jesus Christ's principles and all other moral teaching: Jesus bases everything on God-realisation, while other teachers base everything on self-realisation.

—*Oswald Chambers*[1]

PRAYER

Merciful God, who sent your messengers the prophets to preach repentance and prepare the way for our salvation: Give us grace to heed their warnings and forsake our sins, that we may greet with joy the coming of Jesus Christ our Redeemer; who lives and reigns with you and the Holy Spirit, one God, now and for ever. Amen.[2]

DISCIPLINE (RESPONSE)

Can you identify a current place of conflict in your life? What would God have you do to work at peacemaking in this situation? What truth needs to be spoken in love? What grace needs to be given, perhaps through active listening? The attitude "It's none of my business" does not fly in the Christian life. A significant part of our work is to announce grace and peace everywhere we go.

BLESSING

May the Lord grant you favor with those who are in conflict. May God bless you to offer grace and truth in the manner of Jesus. May the Spirit help you to be a peacemaker everywhere you go. And may the grace and peace of Christ be with you.

❁ Monday in the Third Week of Lent

BIBLE TEXT
Matthew 5:13

CONSIDER

Occasionally we hear people say, "You need to practice what you preach." No one was more concerned about "practicing what he preached" than was Jesus. His message of grace and mercy were consistent with his actions of love and acceptance. I suspect we who call ourselves Christ followers recognize that our mission is to bear witness to Christ.

However, I wonder if our understanding of this is a bit confused. Our first calling is not to *give* a witness. Our first calling is to *be* a witness in a way that comes out of our very nature. Unfortunately, there are plenty of Christians who talk a lot about God but do not live their faith with the same vitality. They speak about God's love, but their lives lack love. These are the examples the world loves to use in discrediting the followers of Jesus. You know the word: "hypocrites." For the watching world it is difficult to separate the message from the messengers.

Jesus knew, of course, that what we *do* emerges from who we *are*. Our *being* precedes our *doing*. So it is intriguing that before Jesus ever gives us a command to do something, he tells us who we are. "You are the salt of the earth." He does not say, "You *should* be" or "It would be nice if you would be"; instead, he says, "You are! You are the salt of the earth." We have to *be* something before we can *do* something. Jesus chooses an interesting metaphor. Salt basically has three purposes: (1) seasoning, to give flavor to something; (2) preservative, to keep things from rotting; and (3) purifying, it can clean and even disinfect. Salt is made to be salty. And if salt isn't salty, it isn't much use—it has no other purpose. If salt loses its tang, you may as well throw it out.

Jesus does not say, "I want you to *become* salty." He says, "You *are* salt by virtue of who you are." His challenge is not to become salty; it is to stay salty. Jesus is saying to us, in effect, "You have a purpose. You are what gives life flavor. In all of the disease sin has brought into life, you are the preserving element. You are to be a cleansing agent in the middle of a dirty world. Your lives are to make people thirsty for God."

READING

Some modern teachers seem to think our Lord said, "Ye are the *sugar* of the earth," meaning that gentleness and winsomeness without curativeness is the ideal of the Christian. Our Lord's illustration of a Christian is salt, and salt is the most concentrated thing known. Salt preserves wholesomeness and prevents decay. It is a disadvantage to be salt. Think of the action of salt on a wound, and you will realise this. If you get salt into a wound, it hurts, and when God's children are amongst those who are "raw" towards God, their presence hurts. The man who is wrong with God is like an open wound, and when "salt" gets in, it causes annoyance and distress and he is spiteful and bitter. The disciples of Jesus in the present dispensation preserve society from corruption; the "salt" causes excessive irritation which spells persecution for the saint.

—Oswald Chambers[3]

PRAYER

Lord, grant that your church may be a true reflection of the kingdom of God. Save us from ordering our lives according to the priorities of this world, and give us the strength and grace to live together as a sign of your mercy, forgiveness, and healing power. Grant this through our Lord Jesus Christ and for the sake of our needy world. Amen.

DISCIPLINE (RESPONSE)

When is the last time someone, noticing your life, asked you, "What is it about you? There is something different about you. What is it?" If this is not happening, it may reveal an area of needed growth in your discipleship. What would it mean to become "salty" so that your life has an impact on the people you encounter day after day?

BLESSING

May the power of the Spirit be upon you today to make your life the flavorful, preserving, and purifying influence in this world that Jesus desires you to be. May the quality of your life, the fruit of the Spirit in you, bear witness to the transforming power of God. And may the peace of our Lord be with you.

● Tuesday in the Third Week of Lent

BIBLE TEXT
Matthew 5:14-16

CONSIDER

In the Beatitudes, previously considered, Jesus gives nine statements of fact before he gets to the verses about being salt and light. Then in these verses, before he says "let your light shine" (v. 16), Jesus tells us who we are. What we *do* is driven by the transformation of who we are. This truth becomes very important and practical for how we live in this world.

Do you know what most people we encounter would like to know about our faith in Jesus? They want to know whether it makes any difference in our lives. They in turn wonder whether it would make any difference for them. If they see us just as frustrated and stressed out and under pressure as they are, then why do they need Jesus? Most of them don't really care how we act when everything is going great. What they are watching closely is how we stand up under pressure. How do we respond with tough decisions? What difference does our integrity make when our values aren't very popular? People want to know if our faith in Jesus makes any practical difference. The truth is, it doesn't make any difference unless Jesus Christ so fills and consumes our lives that there can be no doubt to anyone what we are all about.

Have you ever been in total darkness when you literally could not see your hand in front of your face? It is disorienting and confusing. Have you ever struck a match in the darkness, especially when you're with a group of people? Every head turns immediately to the light. Light is attractive; it has a drawing power. Did you ever sit around a campfire at night? Look around sometime. You will notice that every face in that circle is staring directly into the flames of the fire. Light is captivating.

Jesus said, "You are the light of the world" (v. 14). He also said, "I am the light of the world" (John 8:12). Now he says, "I will shine through you" (see Matt. 5:16). Being light in the world means in part there is correspondence between our words and our conduct. If Jesus is the true Light, then we become light to our world by doing the things that Jesus would do as Jesus shines through us. We are to be so attractive by our joy, our peace, and our love that we draw people to Christ.

READING

In the religion of ancient Israel it was assumed that God was not only the source of light for daily life ("Thy word is a lamp to my feet and a light to my path," Ps. 119:105) but light itself ("in thy light do we see light," Ps. 36:9). This is made more explicit by a New Testament writer: "God is light and in him is no darkness at all" (I John 1:5). Whereas Torah was seen as the primary mediation of God's light by rabbinic Judaism, Christians quickly ascribed this role to Jesus: "I am the light of the world" (John 8:12). Paul declared that he had glimpsed "the light of the knowledge of the glory of God in the face of Christ" (II Cor. 4:6).

In what sense, then, can the church be described as the light of the world? In a derived sense only. It is only as the church genuinely proclaims Christ as Lord . . . that the church can truly be the light of the world (cf. II Cor. 4:5).

—*Douglas Hare*[4]

PRAYER

We beseech Thee, O Lord, let our hearts be graciously enlightened by Thy holy radiance, that we may serve Thee without fear in holiness and righteousness all the days of our life; that so we may escape the darkness of this world, and by Thy guidance attain the land of eternal brightness; through Thy mercy, O blessed Lord, Who dost live and govern all things, world without end. Amen.[5]

DISCIPLINE (RESPONSE)

As you walk through this new day, ask the Spirit to help you be mindful and aware of what you are communicating through your countenance, your words, and your bearing in all things. Is your life reflecting the light of Jesus as you go?

BLESSING

Go into this day bearing the light of God through the Spirit of Jesus Christ, who indwells you by faith. May the light of Christ shine through you. And may the peace of Christ be with you.

❂ Wednesday in the Third Week of Lent

BIBLE TEXT

Matthew 5:17-19

CONSIDER

This Sermon on the Mount is Jesus talking about what it means to be a true disciple. It started so well. We have essentially heard Jesus say, "The real followers in my book are those who are poor in spirit, who mourn and are meek, the merciful and the peacemakers." We hear that disciple-ship has first to do with our attitudes, not our outward actions. This sounds good, and it sounds filled with grace.

About the time we are settling comfortably into this newfound freedom of grace, however, we hear a different word from the lips of the Savior. Now he seems to say, "Don't think for a minute that I am throwing the rules out the window. How you live on the outside, how you order your life, still does matter." In fact, he will say next, "Unless your righteousness exceeds that of the scribes and Pharisees, you will never enter the kingdom of heaven" (v. 20).

Jesus does not dismiss the importance of living upright and holy lives. He says nothing to dismiss the law. Rather, Jesus invites us to go from religion that is outward conformity to the law to an inward purity that results in a truly holy life. There is no doubt that we are not saved by our good works but by grace alone through faith in Christ. At the same time, if our salvation does not bear the fruit of righteousness, it is in danger of withering and dying. Grace has not come so we can live however we want to live. Grace has come so we truly can be holy and righteous.

It is only as we take seriously the call of God to be holy that we can fully experience the grace of God that gives the power to live a holy life. This is when the gospel becomes good news, because here we see that Jesus has done and is doing for us what we cannot do for ourselves. Thanks be to God! If the demand of Jesus was anything less than holiness, then religion would be all our doing. Because he calls us to have righteousness that surpasses that of the Pharisees, we are brought face-to-face every day with our absolute dependency upon his power and grace.

READING

People often think of Christian morality as a kind of bargain in which God says, "If you keep a lot of rules I'll reward you, and if you don't I'll do the other thing." I do not think that is the best way of looking at it. I would much rather say that every time you make a choice you are turning the central part of you, the part of you that chooses, into something a little different from what it was before. And taking your life as a whole, with all your innumerable choices, all your life long you are slowly turning this central thing either into a heavenly creature or into a hellish creature: either into a creature that is in harmony with God, and with other creatures, and with itself, or else into one that is in a state of war and hatred with God, and with its fellow-creatures, and with itself.

—C. S. Lewis[6]

PRAYER

O Sovereign and Almighty Lord, grant that we may end our lives as Christians, acceptable to you and without sin. Be pleased to give us part and lot with all your saints. Pardon all our sins in your abundant and unsearchable goodness, through the grace, mercy, and love of your only begotten Son, through whom and with whom be glory and power to you, with the all-holy, good, and life-giving Spirit. Amen.[7]

DISCIPLINE (RESPONSE)

An important question for personal reflection today may be to ask, "To what degree is my life in Jesus truly bearing the fruit of righteousness?" Are there any points of compromise or bargaining with the world that need to be confessed and, by the help of God, eliminated? Here is where the assistance of a trusted accountability partner can become a valuable asset to your spiritual growth. Is there someone in your life who will tell you the truth about whether or not there seems to be agreement between your profession of faith and the living out of your faith?

BLESSING

May the grace and strength of the Lord be with you today, aiding you in the integrity of a life that is a true reflection of the presence of Christ Jesus. And may the peace of Christ be with you.

❂ Thursday in the Third Week of Lent

BIBLE TEXT

Matthew 5:20

CONSIDER

How good do we have to be? According to Jesus, we have to be better than the religious professionals. The Pharisees have been beaten up pretty badly for their image, but these were really good folks. Some preachers and teachers have noted that whenever we read "Pharisee" in the Bible, we should probably just go ahead and insert our names. Pharisees were very careful to do the right things. They knew the Scriptures, they lived by the book, and they kept themselves clean. These were people who would eventually cry out, "Crucify him!" Why would good people say such a thing? It was because Jesus, who had just said he wasn't about to abolish the law (which pleased these conservative folks), turned right around and seemed to do just that.

"Why does your teacher eat with tax collectors and sinners?" the scribes and Pharisees asked (9:11). It was a clear violation of the law. "I came not to call the righteous, but sinners," replied Jesus (v. 13).

"The Pharisees fast, so why don't your people fast?" they wanted to know (see v. 14). And Jesus said, "Doesn't the wedding party begin when the bridegroom shows up? Forget your rules about fasting, let the party begin!" (see v. 15).

"Look," they said, "your disciples are doing what it's not lawful to do on the Sabbath!" (see Mark 2:24). And he said, "The Sabbath was made for man, not man for the Sabbath" (v. 27).

This is our Jesus. On the one hand, he is saying, "You've got to be more holy than the religious professionals." But on the other hand, he says, "Listen, you can be so right that you're wrong. You can be so religious that you miss the point of religion. Legalism can just suck the life out of religion until it is cold and calculating."

This brings to mind the old adage that some people are so heavenly minded that they are no earthly good. The message of this saying is not about playing fast and loose with the holy life to which God calls us. The message has to do with the profound recognition that the only way we can stand before God with "clean hands and a pure heart" (Ps. 24:4) is not by our religious efforts but by the loving mercy of God, who through Jesus offers us the joy of a transformed life.

READING

Is it too strong to call this a spiritual torpedo? These statements of Jesus are the most revolutionary statements human ears ever listened to, and it needs the Holy Ghost to interpret them to us; the shallow admiration for Jesus Christ as a Teacher that is taught today is of no use.

Who is going to climb that "hill of the Lord"? To stand before God and say, "My hands are clean, my heart is pure"—who can do it? Who can stand in the Eternal light of God and have nothing for God to blame in him? Only the Son of God; and if the Son of God is formed in us by regeneration and sanctification, He will exhibit Himself through our mortal flesh. That is the ideal of Christianity, "that the life also of Jesus might be made manifest in our mortal flesh."

—Oswald Chambers[8]

PRAYER

Almighty and everlasting God, you hate nothing that you have made, and forgive the sins of all those who are penitent. Create and make in us new and contrite hearts, that, lamenting our sins and acknowledging our wretchedness, we may receive from you, the God of all mercy, perfect forgiveness and peace; through Jesus Christ our Lord. Amen.[9]

DISCIPLINE (RESPONSE)

This is a season for fasting. If we are not careful, our fasting can become a religious work whereby we seek or even expect the favor of God because of our discipline. True fasting rises not from a fearful heart but from a grateful heart as a natural response to our complete dependency upon God. As you fast during this season, invite the Holy Spirit to show you the motivation for your fasting. Is it fear or is it love?

BLESSING

May God's command "You shall be holy, for I am holy" (1 Pet. 1:16) be accomplished in your life by the abundant grace of God in Christ. And may the peace of our Lord Jesus Christ be with you.

❀ Friday in the Third Week of Lent

BIBLE TEXT

Matthew 5:21-22

CONSIDER

Now Jesus really gets nosy and begins rummaging around in the base-
ment of the heart, digging up things like anger. "Everyone who is angry
with his brother will be liable to judgment," he says (v. 22). Come on,
you've got to be kidding. Who isn't angry with his or her brother (or sister)
at some point? Anger is just a part of life, isn't it? We can't help it if people
make us angry, can we? We see the results of anger every day of our lives.
We all know what it is to experience anger.

Jesus goes right into the heart of this basic emotion and says in effect,
"True Christianity makes a difference right there." To be clear, anger itself
is not sinful. What is at stake here is that even powerful emotions such as
anger are brought under the control of Jesus Christ. The hard truth about
anger is that it so easily gives way to sin. Anger can quickly turn to choices
that are in no way consistent with life in the kingdom of God.

Contemporary culture reinforces the idea that we all have a right to
anger and the expression of it. We think we should be able to vent our
anger, and if people get hurt in the process, it is only because they are
being sensitive. This is precisely the kind of attitude Jesus is confronting.
His concern is whether or not we murder with our words, tone of voice,
and attitudes. What Jesus condemns here is abusive language—words
that tear down, hurt, and devalue another human being.

"Whoever insults his brother will be liable to the council" (v. 22). The
word is *raca*, a word that means "empty headed" and "good for nothing."
It would not seem as grievous as actually murdering a person. The truth
is that there is more than one way to kill a person. The lives of innocent
people are taken all the time with words of anger and hate. Some of us
may be guilty of crushing and killing others with our words of anger and
bitterness. Maybe we tell ourselves that it really does not matter that
much. It matters. How we talk to the people in our households and work-
places does matter. The apostle Paul wrote, "Let your speech always be

gracious, seasoned with salt, so that you may know how you ought to answer each person" (Col. 4:6).

READING

Our Lord goes behind the old law to the disposition. Everything He says is impossible unless He can put His Spirit into me and remake me from within, then I begin to see how it can be done. When a man is born from above, he does not need to pretend to be a saint, he cannot help being one.

—*Oswald Chambers*[10]

PRAYER

Almighty, eternal God, Lord of the whole world, the Creator and Governor of all things, we pray for the peace and happy settlement of the world and of the holy churches. Give us your peace that can never be taken away. May you fulfill in us such virtue as is in keeping with godliness. We pray for our enemies and those who hate us. We pray for those who persecute us for the name of the Lord. . . . Preserve us for your heavenly kingdom. Save us, and lift us up, O God, by your mercy. . . . Amen.[11]

DISCIPLINE (RESPONSE)

Is there a circumstance or a relationship in your life that has become characterized by anger? Are you being tempted to use harsh and hurtful words in response to the situation or person? Perhaps your focus today would be upon surrendering the situation or the relationship to God. What if you were to trust God completely to take care of this matter? Can you begin to sense the peace of Christ replacing the stress of your anger?

BLESSING

May the peace of God in Christ so envelop you that anger gives way to compassion, and revenge is traded for blessing. May the Lord deliver you from the temptation to nurse anger and help you to release it to him. May the grace and peace of our Lord stand guard over your heart and mind this day.

❁ Saturday in the Third Week of Lent

BIBLE TEXT
Matthew 5:23-26

CONSIDER

Here Jesus confronts us with the reality that how we treat others has a direct impact on our worship. He seems to say, "If there is bitterness and anger between you and another person, if there have been hurtful words, don't you dare come to the sanctuary and pretend that everything is okay. You go and make it right, or your worship means nothing." If we really want to put Jesus first in our lives, then we will discover that he insists we put others first.

Our relationships with one another are always in view when we come before God in worship. Fractured relationships inhibit our ability to bring an acceptable gift of worship to the Lord. The issue of who was in the wrong or who harmed whom is really beside the point here. Broken relationships cripple the vitality of the church because too many of us are waiting for the other person to make the first move. The Jesus way is to take the initiative, to make the first move toward reconciliation and peace.

Following the 1995 bombing of the Alfred P. Murrah Federal Building in Oklahoma City, a citywide memorial service was held. Billy Graham spoke in that service, and among his comments were words about forgiveness. Not many across the nation were ready to think of forgiveness. Dr. Graham was suggesting something that is peculiar to a faith that teaches us to pray, "Forgive us our sins as we forgive those who sin against us."[12] Forgiveness can seem a scandalous response to the abuses we sometimes suffer. Yet there it is at the heart of the gospel, calling us to lay down our rights and move toward one another from the very impulse that moves God toward us.

To speak plainly: it is not enough for us to be reconciled to God and at odds with our brother or sister. These words of Jesus are making this point clearly: "First be reconciled to your brother, and then come and offer your gift" (v. 24). So, who are we at odds with today? Who are we experiencing a broken relationship with today? Reconciliation is a two-way street, but where there is strife, mistrust, and unforgiveness in a relationship, have we done everything we could do to restore that relationship? Have we been willing to embrace the scandal of forgiveness?

READING

It should be well observed, not only that this is a step which our Lord absolutely commands us to take, but that he commands us to take this step first, before we attempt any other. No alternative is allowed, no choice of anything else: This is the way; walk thou in it. It is true, he enjoins us, if need require, to take two other steps; but they are to be taken successively after this step, and neither of them before it: Much less are we to take any other step, either before or beside this. To do anything else, or not to do this, is, therefore, equally inexcusable.

—*John Wesley*[13]

PRAYER

Almighty Father, whose blessed Son before his passion prayed for his disciples that they might be one, as you and he are one: Grant that your Church, being bound together in love and obedience to you, may be united in one body by the one Spirit, that the world may believe in him whom you have sent, your Son Jesus Christ our Lord; who lives and reigns with you, in the unity of the Holy Spirit, one God, now and for ever. Amen.[14]

DISCIPLINE (RESPONSE)

Would the Lord bring to mind today a relationship that is broken? A good and beautiful act of worship in this Lenten season may involve taking the initiative prayerfully to reconcile with your brother or sister. Your prayer today for grace and courage to do this will be met with the abundant resources of a God who always moves toward us with mercy, forgiveness, and love.

BLESSING

May the Lord bless you today with courage to face the most difficult relationship of your life. May the powerful and redeeming grace of God breathe new life into that which the world would count for dead. And may your worship be true as you forgive as one forgiven. The peace of our Lord be with you.

* The Fourth Week of Lent
(Third Sunday to Day 22)

✸ Third Sunday in Lent

BIBLE TEXT

Matthew 5:27-28

CONSIDER

When the subject turns to sex, particularly in church, usually things get very quiet and serious. There is not a person in the church or in the whole world for whom sexuality is not an important issue. Jesus knew that sexuality grabs our attention because it lies at the very heart of how God made us. God made us for intimacy, and God made sex for the expression of that intimacy between a husband and a wife. But Jesus also knew the world in which we live and that this wonderful creation of God has been twisted and turned inward.

Jesus is talking to us about what it means to be authentically Christian. These words about adultery and lust follow the same pattern as the words about murder and anger. "You think you're doing well if you don't commit adultery." Most of us could probably offer the Lord a pretty clean slate on this count. But because we can, we tend to cut ourselves an awful lot of slack for what goes on in the private places of our minds and hearts. Jesus doesn't let us get away with that if we want to be serious followers of him.

"I say to you that everyone who looks at a woman with lustful intent has already committed adultery with her in his heart" (v. 28). Jesus goes right to the heart of men who (in that time and culture) would never be considered adulterers but who were full of inappropriate sexual desire. Jesus says to them, "It's not enough that you can stand within the legal limits. I want to know what goes on in your mind and heart."

More than likely when Jesus begins asking these kinds of questions none of us feels too righteous. What is lust, really? Lust is not the feeling that arises when we find ourselves attracted to a member of the opposite sex. Lust, as Jesus condemns it here, is a sexual attitude and mind-set that places self-gratification over intimacy with the beloved (in the context of marriage). Lust is an out-of-touch desire for something or someone that is not yours. Perhaps this is why Jesus uses this poignant example to speak of what it means to be truly Christian. An authentically Christian person always puts the value and dignity of people above personal satisfaction.

READING

Married or single, purity calls us to the highest regard for others, to see them as persons and not as bodies to be used for our pleasure. However, marriage is a covenant. Jesus expects His disciples to keep covenant in both deed and attitude. When two persons covenant to be husband and wife, for one to entertain thoughts of relating sexually to someone other than the spouse, makes that one guilty of breaking covenant. Such would have committed adultery against the spouse, if even only in thought. This is the highest standard of fidelity in marriage!

—*Myron S. Augsburger*[1]

PRAYER

Holy Ghost, with light divine,
Shine upon this heart of mine!
Chase the shades of night away,
Turn the darkness into day.

. . . .

Holy Spirit, all divine,
Dwell within this heart of mine;
Cast down ev'ry idol throne,
Reign supreme, and reign alone.[2] *Amen.*

DISCIPLINE (RESPONSE)

Many people have been helped through the direction of twelve-step programs. In that system the fourth step is usually stated, "Make a searching and fearless moral inventory of ourselves."[3] Perhaps it's a good idea to begin such an inventory during this fourth week of Lent. Can you be ruthlessly honest about the condition of your mind when it comes to lust? To what degree are you allowing your mind-set in this regard to be shaped by a hypersexualized culture?

BLESSING

As you go into a world driven by the "desires of the flesh and the desires of the eyes and pride of life" (1 John 2:16), may the grace of God be poured out upon your life to strengthen you for love and purity in a fearful and sin-marred world. May the peace of Jesus Christ be with you.

❂ Monday in the Fourth Week of Lent

BIBLE TEXT
Matthew 5:29-30

CONSIDER

In his confrontation of our propensity toward lust Jesus goes even further. Now he says that in order to honor God in this area of life we may have to become willing to take drastic measures. Clearly Jesus is not advocating self-mutilation. He's getting our attention, and the intent of his words *does* need to be taken literally. The intent is fairly simple: Are you willing to take drastic measures to honor God and be pure and holy in the area of sexuality? How serious are you about following Christ?

If you are being tempted by a coworker and find yourself considering the possibility of engaging in an inappropriate relationship, what are you willing to do to get free of that lust? Are you willing to quit your job and get away from that person? Doesn't that seem to be what Jesus is getting at? Gouge out your eye, cut off your hand, quit your job—sometimes it's necessary to take drastic measures.

If your job takes you on the road often and you find yourself being constantly drawn toward lustful thoughts and behaviors, what are you willing to do to get free from that? Are you willing to get rid of the cable television? Are you willing to take drastic measures to help maintain your integrity in your use of the Internet? If you are addicted to pornography, are you willing to confess your addiction and get it out in the open? Taking such measures may seem drastic, but can you say that this is not what Jesus is talking about? Do not misunderstand the core issue; this is all about your heart. It ultimately doesn't matter if you seem to be holy on the outside. What really matters is what you and God know is real on the inside.

READING

Your right hand is . . . one of the best things you have, but Jesus says if it offends you in developing your spiritual life, and hinders you in following His precepts, cut it off and cast it from you. Jesus Christ spoke rugged truth, . . . and He says it is better to be maimed than damned, better to enter into life lame in man's sight and lovely in God's than to be lovely in man's sight and lame in God's. It is a maimed life to begin with, such as Jesus describes in these verses; otherwise we may look all right in the sight of our fellow men, but be remarkably twisted and wrong in the sight of God.

—*Oswald Chambers*[4]

PRAYER

O blessed and all-redeeming blood, which flowed so freely from the source of life,

Bathe our polluted souls in thy clear streams, and purge away all our foul impurities.

Cleanse us, O merciful Lord, from our secret faults, and from those darling sins that most abuse us.

Wash off the stains our malice has caused in others, and those which our weakness has received of them.

Let not them perish by our occasions, nor us be undone by theirs.

But let our charity assist one another, and thy clemency pardon us all.

Pardon, O gracious Jesus, what we have been; with thy holy discipline correct what we are!

Order by thy providence what we shall be; and, in the end, crown thine own gifts. Amen.[5]

DISCIPLINE (RESPONSE)

Drastic measures of spiritual discipline should only be undertaken with much prayer and with wise spiritual counsel. If God is speaking to you about a drastic measure that you think may serve your holiness, seek out a mature and trusted counselor in whom you can confide your thought. And should the Lord confirm your sensing, ask someone to walk with you through the steps of obedience. The Comforter, the Holy Spirit, will guide you into all truth.

BLESSING

May the grace of the Lord be upon you to discern clearly the voice of the Holy Spirit in these matters. May God grant you a passionate desire to be holy in your innermost being. And may you know, by faith, the cleansing power of the Spirit to sanctify you for the purposes of God in this world. The peace of Christ be with you.

❋ Tuesday in the Fourth Week of Lent

BIBLE TEXT

Matthew 5:31-32

CONSIDER

Later in Matthew's gospel (chap. 19) Jesus will engage the Pharisees again on this matter of divorce. The Pharisees questioned Jesus, not to learn, but to somehow trap him in his words. The acknowledgment of Jesus here about a "certificate of divorce" reaches to Deuteronomy 24, where there is provision in the law of Moses. Jesus said, "Moses gave you that provision, not because that's what God designed, but because your hearts are hard. You are set against God's will." Then Jesus said, "If you really want to know what God thinks about divorce, don't go to Deuteronomy 24; go to Genesis. Let's talk about what God originally had in mind" (see Matt. 19:3-8).

The primary concern of the Jews was their rights and what they could get by with. The primary concern of Jesus was the will of God. Not much has changed has it? So much of our conversation about divorce comes from just that kind of self-willed perspective. What are my rights? What can I get away with and still be okay with God? What will make me happy?

Jesus means to press God's intention for marriage into the compromised hearts of these folks. The law to which they appeal is nothing more than God's gracious provision (for the women who had no social rights) in response to their sin of divorcing their wives for all manner of selfish reasons. Jesus also acknowledges that while divorce is never the will of God, it is sometimes permitted as a divine concession to the human hardness of heart. The only reason God ever allows divorce is to keep us from doing our very worst to each other. When there are situations of abuse, sinfulness, and danger, it may serve no redemptive purpose for that situation to continue. But although God allows it, God never approves. The worst thing that Christians could do is to exercise the gracious concession of God to our sinfulness and then somehow call it God's good will for our lives. The will of God for the marriage relationship is that we are to "cleave" to one another and become "one flesh" (Gen.

2:24; Matt. 19:5, KJV). Once again Jesus refuses to allow us to slip by with mere adherence to the rules. He is saying to us that authentic discipleship changes our hearts and as a result changes our lives.

READING

This expression of the consequences of divorce would surely have a stunning effect on the contemporary Jewish mind. To begin with, it would have involved an earthquake in their evaluation of women. In legal terms women did not count. Jesus' declaration that remarriage following divorce was tantamount to adultery would have been even more stunning. . . . divorce was an accepted institution in Judaism. The only disagreement was in regard to the grounds on which it was permissible. This appears to have been precisely the point of Jesus' critique. The real matter for debate was not on what grounds divorce should be permissible but whether divorce was permissible at all.

—Alex R. G. Deasley[6]

PRAYER

O God, who hast taught us to keep all thy commandments by loving thee and our neighbor: Grant us the grace of thy Holy Spirit, that we may be devoted to thee with our whole heart, and united to one another with pure affection; through Jesus Christ our Lord, who liveth and reigneth with thee and the same Spirit, one God, for ever and ever. Amen.[7]

DISCIPLINE (RESPONSE)

If you are married, pray today for your marriage that your relationship may become an authentic reflection of the kingdom of God in this world. Listen carefully for anything the Spirit might teach you about how to love your spouse more. If you are unmarried, pray for the married couples whom you love, that the spouses may not only be faithful to their vows but also model the joy of serving one another in Jesus' name.

BLESSING

As you go into this new day, may the Lord save you from the false values of this broken world. May the Spirit unmask the attractive but deadly posture of self-centeredness. And may God help you to lay down your life in service to another. Grace and peace to you from God our Father and the Lord Jesus Christ.

❃ Wednesday in the Fourth Week of Lent

BIBLE TEXT

Matthew 5:33-37

CONSIDER

Jesus speaks to some people who had learned to manipulate the concept of truth speaking to fit comfortably into their lives. Now these folks would have no doubt said they were committed to truth speaking and probably really believed they were people of truth, but in fact they had compartmentalized things, telling the truth over here and playing fast and loose with it over there. They knew very well what the law said. Leviticus 19:12 says plainly, "You shall not swear by my name falsely." They took this seriously, but to get around it they began to "swear" by other things. If you swore an oath by the name of God, you were stuck. But if you swore by heaven, the earth, Jerusalem, or even your own head, you could lead folks to believe you were committed to truth telling, but in a pinch it wasn't really binding.

Into this kind of silliness Jesus speaks a very simple word. He basically says to them and to us, "Why don't you forget all that 'technical loophole' stuff and just be a person who speaks the truth? Let your simple 'yes' mean 'yes' and your simple 'no' really mean 'no.'"

How is it with you when it comes to being a person of truthfulness? Are you the kind of person that people trust? Are you known as a person of your word? What Jesus wants to do for every one of us is take away the need to self-protect and manipulate our relationships. He wants to give us the freedom to live such a simple and honest life that in our speech and in our dealings with people our "yes" can simply mean "yes" and our "no" can simply mean "no." You cannot even begin to live like this until you allow Jesus to come into your life and have complete control. And if you are a Christian, you can't be like this unless you have learned the secret of living in daily surrender to the lordship of Jesus Christ. What truth would Jesus speak to you today about his call to you to be a truth speaker?

READING

The prohibition of oaths and the demand that simply one's word stand for itself is nothing less than to demand a relationship between individuals characterized by total honesty. This call for total honesty comes through most clearly in the tradition of James 5:12, where one's "yes" means "yes" and one's "no" means "no." Matthew has captured this different starting point. . . . "Anything more than one's word is of the Evil One." . . . Therefore, Jesus' demand, set once again in the context of the Law, cuts to the heart of the human predicament. Whereas the Law assumes dishonesty to be a given and forbids swearing a false oath, Jesus forbids the use of any false word at all. Such a demand presupposes the context of total honesty in human relationships.

—*Robert A. Guelich*[8]

PRAYER

Take thou the full possession of my heart; raise there thy throne, and command there as thou dost in heaven. Being created by thee, let me live to thee; being created for thee, let me ever act for thy glory; being redeemed by thee, let me render unto thee what is thine, and let my spirit ever cleave to thee alone. Amen.[9]

DISCIPLINE (RESPONSE)

Is there such integrity in your speech that you never have to worry that what was said to one person is different from what was spoken to another? In your mind, go back over yesterday's events. Are you willing to stand by everything you said and everything you wrote? If not, ask the Lord to show you why sometimes you are afraid to speak the truth.

BLESSING

May your "mouth" speak "what is true" (Prov. 8:7, NIV), and may you know the peaceful integrity of speech that matches your heart. Receive the grace of God to be true in your speech, and may the peace of Christ be with you.

❀ Thursday in the Fourth Week of Lent

BIBLE TEXT

Matthew 5:38-42

CONSIDER

"Do unto others exactly what they do to you."

"It's not a threat; it's a promise."

"I don't get mad; I just get even."

"I'll make her sorry she ever said that."

Any of these thoughts ever cross your mind in a moment of anger? Any of these words ever slip out of your mouth when feelings of vengeance welled up within? We know about the feelings of revenge and retaliation, don't we? Words like these are some of the hardest in the New Testament. They are also some of the most misquoted, misused, and abused words in the Scriptures. How many times have you heard the "eye for an eye" statement quoted as a justification for revenge? Clearly the context of Jesus' words in verses 38-42 is far different from that. Even the Old Testament context of this law was trying to promote restraint. Things were so out of hand that the old law was *"Only an eye for an eye and only a tooth for a tooth"* (see Exod. 21:24; Lev. 24:20; Deut. 19:21). But Jesus takes the law to a whole new level.

"Do not resist the one who is evil" (Matt. 5:39). Is he serious? Does he mean that when someone wrongfully uses me, I'm just supposed to let the person do it? "If anyone slaps you on the right cheek, turn to him the other also" (v. 39). What is Jesus really trying to get at here? Remember, he's talking about the basics of what it means to be Christian. These are not the super add-ons for the very holy. He is saying that this kind of attitude is and must be resident in the heart of every true believer. When the temptation comes for retaliation and when the opportunity arises for vengeance, Jesus says the Christian goes another way.

Jesus calls us to lay down our rights and to fulfill our responsibilities. Surely we can see turning the other cheek and going the second mile for those who are in our families or perhaps in our little Christian group. That's not who Jesus is talking about here. He is talking about doing these things for those who are enemies. In fact, he goes on to say that if we love only those who love us in return, we are nothing special. Pagans know how to do that. Jesus calls us to something unique and profound, the unbelievable ability to love those who don't belong and to love those who are a pain in the neck.

READING

If a disciple is going to follow Jesus Christ, he must lay his account not only with purity and with practice, but also with persecution. The picture our Lord gives is not familiar to us. In the East, a slap on the cheek is the greatest form of insult; its equivalent with us would be spitting in the face. Epictetus, a Roman slave, said that a slave would rather be thrashed to death than flicked on the cheek. Jesus says, "If any man shall smite thee on the right cheek, turn to him the other also." The Sermon on the Mount indicates that when we are on Jesus Christ's errands, no time is to be taken in standing up for ourselves. Personal insult will be an occasion in the saint for revealing the incredible sweetness of the Lord Jesus.

—*Oswald Chambers*[10]

PRAYER

Our Father, we confess that we prefer to love those who love us. Teach us to love as you love. Help us especially when our love is challenged by the adversarial actions of another. Grant us grace to lay down our lives in service even to those who would be our enemies. For the sake of Christ who died for us while we were enemies, we pray. Amen.

DISCIPLINE (RESPONSE)

Think of a time as recent as possible when you were treated poorly. What were the thoughts and feelings that came into your mind and heart? What did you actually do? Perhaps you are facing some kind of mistreatment even now. Have you brought the injustice to the Lord? What might God say to you about what a Christlike response to this unfair treatment may look like?

BLESSING

May the grace of God our Father and the Lord Jesus Christ be with you in all circumstances of this day. May the peace of Christ by the Spirit follow you in every situation and hold you securely in God's love. And may you, by the grace of God, respond to every unkind word and action with the love of Christ, who is your Defender and your Peace.

❋ Friday in the Fourth Week of Lent

BIBLE TEXT
Matthew 5:43-45

CONSIDER
There is only one way to live out the incredible imperatives of yesterday's text. One thing makes this way of living credible and doable. It's what Jesus talks about in these verses. It is love. Of course when Jesus says that love is the key to living this way, we are not speaking of warm feelings but of actions. This kind of love is something we do. It rises from a commitment to see God's very best happen in the life of every person, including our enemies.

This kind of love is not something we manufacture. This is God's love that he has given to us. Now we are called to share this love with those around us. Love does crazy things, such as turning the other cheek and choosing to forgive when it would be so easy to hold a grudge. Love reaches out to others when everything in us wants to avoid them. Love treats people better than they deserve to be treated. Love is patient; it is able to see beyond the immediate hurt to what is really happening in the life of the person who seems so against us. By the way, do you realize that enemies can sometimes really help us? Sometimes our "enemies" are right in their opposition to us. What they say is hard, and perhaps they could say it in a better spirit and attitude, but we may need to hear their words. God knows this, and it is why he does not want us writing our enemies off.

But how in the world could a person ever really live this way in the real world? Jesus seems to give us two directives. One is implicit: he says that this is the way we are as children of the Father. In other words, treating people like this needs to become not so much a function of discipline but a matter of character. This is just what Christians do. It can become the normal response of those who have surrendered their lives to the control of Jesus as Lord. The second directive is explicit: Jesus tells us to pray for those who make life hard on us. "Love your enemies and pray for those who persecute you" (v. 44). How are we to pray? Do we pray that they will be changed? Perhaps, but maybe more than anything this points to the reality that in prayer we begin to see them as God sees them.

READING

The basis for Jesus' audacious command to love our enemies is that such is God's own nature. Loving our enemies qualifies us to be counted as authentic children of our **Father in heaven**. . . . The illustrations of God's love for enemies instruct us regarding Jesus' meaning. God's love for enemies is shown by the fact that He grants sunshine to **the evil and the good**. God **sends rain on the righteous and the unrighteous**. In the basic necessities of life, God does not discriminate between those who love Him and those who hate Him. The Greek word used for love is *agape*, which means to seek the best for the other. God gives the good gifts of sun and rain to people regardless of their response to Him.

—*Roger Hahn*[11]

PRAYER

O God, the Father of all, whose Son commanded us to love our enemies: Lead them and us from prejudice to truth; deliver them and us from hatred, cruelty, and revenge; and in your good time enable us all to stand reconciled before you; through Jesus Christ our Lord. Amen.[12]

DISCIPLINE (RESPONSE)

Whom would you count as an enemy today? Are you able to name specifically what he or she has done to become an enemy to you? Is there anything about what he or she has done or is saying that could carry a measure of truth from which you need to learn? Pray that God will help you not to steel your heart against something you may need to learn, even from an enemy.

BLESSING

May the Lord in his great mercy grant you abundant grace to treat your enemies the way God does. May the Lord grant you strength to surrender to him your desire for vindication. And may the Lord place his love in your heart for those who persecute you. The peace of Jesus be yours.

❋ Saturday in the Fourth Week of Lent

BIBLE TEXT

Matthew 5:46-47

CONSIDER

Jesus knows that this business of loving and praying for our enemies is hard for us. He keeps pressing the point, reminding us that the love we are called to share with our enemies is a love that rises far above the kind of love this world knows. So what do we pray for and what does it really mean to love our enemies in a way that makes us remarkable in a world mostly acquainted with retribution and vengeance?

At the heart of it seems to be something about perspective. It is Jesus' reminder that the love of which we are speaking rises from a perspective different from that with which the world is most familiar. Brennan Manning's take on this was noted earlier but bears repeating here: "Behind men's grumpiest poses and most puzzling defense mechanism, behind their arrogance and airs, behind their silence, sneers, and curses, Jesus saw little children who hadn't been loved enough and who had ceased growing because someone had ceased believing in them."[13] This kind of perspective begins to help us see that the love we are to offer to our enemies has nothing to do with whether or not they deserve the love. In fact, they do not. Nor do we deserve God's love, and this is precisely the point. This is a love that can only be generated by the very Spirit of God, who indwells us by faith.

What Jesus is actually inviting us to do as his followers is to demonstrate through our own lives the very thing that God is up to in this world. "God so loved the world" (John 3:16), all of the world, every person in the world. It is unbelievable and scandalous. It is lavish and foolish to the world's way of judging things. And as God's people we are called to become living signs of this kind of lavish and foolish love that would turn the other cheek, go the extra mile, and shower love upon the very ones who persecute us.

READING

The Bible never speaks vaguely; it always speaks definitely. People speak about loving "mankind," and loving the "heathen"; Jesus says, "Love your enemies." Our Lord does not say, "Bless your enemies"; He says, "Love your enemies." He does not say, "Love them that curse you"; He says, "Bless them that curse you." "Do good to them that hate you,"—not bless them. He does not say, "Do good to them that despitefully use you"; He says, "Pray for them that despitefully use you." Each one of these commands is stamped with sheer impossibility to the natural man. If we reverse the order Jesus has given, it can be done with strain, but kept in His order I defy any man on earth to be able to do it unless he has been regenerated by God the Holy Ghost. When a man does love his enemies, he knows that God has done a tremendous work in him, and everyone else knows it too.

—Oswald Chambers[14]

PRAYER

O Father, calm the turbulence of our passions; quiet the throbbing of our hopes; repress the waywardness of our wills; direct the motions of our affections; and sanctify the varieties of our lot. Be Thou all in all to us; and may all things earthly, while we bend them to our growth in grace, and to the work of blessing, dwell lightly in our hearts, so that we may readily, or even joyfully, give up whatever Thou dost ask for.[15] Amen.

DISCIPLINE (RESPONSE)

Usually we adopt particular ways of looking at our enemies that help to explain to us why they are acting harshly toward us. As you think about those who may be enemies to you, ask the Lord to help you see them in ways you have never seen them before. Pray to God for perspective on why your enemies are acting as they do, and ask the Lord for compassion toward the brokenness of your enemies.

BLESSING

"You, O Lord, are a shield about me, my glory, and the lifter of my head. I cried aloud to the Lord, and he answered me from his holy hill. . . . I lay down and slept; I woke again, for the Lord sustained me. I will not be afraid of many thousands of people who have set themselves against me all around" (Ps. 3:3-6). The peace of Christ be with you.

✳ The Fifth Week of Lent
(Fourth Sunday to Day 28)

✹ Fourth Sunday in Lent

BIBLE TEXT
Matthew 5:48

CONSIDER

All of Jesus' talk about loving enemies and praying for the persecutor is critical and necessary for understanding this most troubling of statements. We immediately recoil at this statement, almost embarrassed that such an imperative was spoken by our Lord. We know that no one is perfect, and this recognition finds its way into our daily conversation. "Well, nobody is perfect," we like to say. However, Jesus is not speaking of perfect performance or flawless behavior in the ways we usually imagine it. Jesus is talking about perfect love, which does not find its origin within us. This is God's perfect love so filling our hearts by the Holy Spirit that it becomes a natural thing for that love to flow out of us, even toward our enemies.

The challenge of this language in English is that we understand the word "perfect" to mean "flawless." The perfection of which Jesus speaks is something like the idea of wholeness. The word in Greek is *teleios*, which can be thought of as fulfilling the purpose for which we were created. This fulfillment of purpose can be fully known even while it is growing and maturing. It is *now* and *not yet*. Imagine a clay water jar of the type that may have been in use during Jesus' time. A jar that is able to contain water is fulfilling its purpose, its *teleios*. Suppose that jar became broken. It would no longer be capable of its *teleios*, its intended purpose. But imagine that someone was able to mend the jar by cementing the pieces back together so that it could once again hold water. It probably would not be flawless; we could no doubt see the cracks where it was once broken, and it may even have a small leak. If, however, the jar is able to fulfill its intended function, it is fulfilling its *teleios*.

Jesus is not calling us to the impossible perfection of a flawless life. He is calling us to fulfill our intended purpose: to love God "with all your heart and with all your soul and with all your mind. . . . And . . . [to] love your neighbor as yourself" (22:37, 39).

READING

There is scarce any expression in holy writ, which has given more offense than this. The word *perfect* is what many cannot bear. The very sound of it is an abomination to them; and whosoever *preaches perfection* (as the phrase is)—that is, asserts that it is attainable in this life—runs great hazard of being accounted by them worse than a heathen man or a publican.

And hence some have advised, wholly to lay aside the use of those expressions; "because they have given so great offense." But are they not found in the oracles [Word] of God? If so, by what authority can any Messenger of God lay them aside, even though all men [and women] should be offended?

—*John Wesley*[1]

PRAYER

Christ be with me, Christ within me,
Christ behind me, Christ before me,
Christ beside me, Christ to win me,
Christ to comfort and restore me,
Christ beneath me, Christ above me,
Christ in quiet, Christ in danger,
Christ in hearts of all that love me,
Christ in mouth of friend and stranger.[2] Amen.

DISCIPLINE (RESPONSE)

Consider what you plan to do today. What will consume your energy, your time, your resources, and your attention? Are you fulfilling the purpose for which you were created? What changes may need to be considered to live out more fully the perfect love of God dwelling within you?

BLESSING

May the perfect love of God be shed abroad in our hearts this day. By the abundant mercies of God, may we fulfill the purpose for which we were created. And may the activities of this day be fully surrendered to the perfect will of God. The peace of our Lord Jesus Christ be with you.

❀ Monday in the Fifth Week of Lent

BIBLE TEXT
Matthew 6:1-4

CONSIDER

The focus of the Sermon on the Mount now shifts a bit to what Jesus calls "your righteousness," or acts of piety. These are the basic things that Christians are expected to do. They follow the Jewish pattern of religious expectation: giving, prayer, and fasting. Jesus does not intend to say that these are the only three disciplines of a Christian, but these are representative of the kinds of things a religious person does. The challenge of this teaching is that righteous acts can be done in the right way or they can be done in the wrong way.

We see clearly in Jesus' words that there is one group of folks who do the right things outwardly, and yet they are condemned. Then there is another group who also do the right things with the right heart, and they are rewarded. The whole thing turns on motive. Why do we do what we do? By the way, Jesus does not exhort us here to be involved in acts of righteousness—he already assumes that we are. To the disciple of Jesus this is as natural as breathing. This is just who we are, and thus it's what we do.

The critical factor here is the phrase "before other people in order to be seen by them" (v. 1). Be careful that your service is not for the purpose of gaining some perceived reward from those who happen to see it or become aware of it. If that is the motive in your service, then whenever someone notices and pats you on the back, you just got all the reward you're ever going to get.

So Jesus says that the way we go about our service is secretly. "Do not let your left hand know what your right hand is doing," he says (v. 3). Of course he is talking in hyperbole to make the point, but evidently what Jesus wants us to get is that one of the marks of a true Christian is quiet service. It's a kind of service where we go about our ministry in obedience to God, using the gifts he has given with no regard for who notices or who doesn't notice. This sounds much easier than it actually is. We are wired to need affirmation. Most of us enjoy recognition and praise. This is not what Jesus warns us against. The issue is whether that need for affirmation and praise has taken over and become the motivating factor in our service.

READING

I try to give to the poor people for love what the rich could get for money. No, I wouldn't touch a leper for a thousand pounds; yet I willingly cure him for the love of God.

—*Mother Teresa of Calcutta*[3]

PRAYER

God, remove from my heart any misplaced desire for the affirmation of others. Let me seek your approval above all others, recognizing that I am approved by your grace, mercy, and love. Help me to be generous in every way that I might glorify you in all things. Amen.

DISCIPLINE (RESPONSE)

A significant act of Lenten discipline may be to make a thorough assessment of your giving. Is there enough evidence to convict you of being a generous person? And what about your motive for giving? How important is it to you that you receive recognition for your generosity? What might the Lord have you do this week to live out the heart of this text?

BLESSING

"God is able to make all grace abound to you, so that having all sufficiency in all things at all times, you may abound in every good work" (2 Cor. 9:8). May the Lord bless you with a generous and humble heart, that you may be a vessel of God's generosity to those around you. The peace of our Lord be with you today.

❀ Tuesday in the Fifth Week of Lent

BIBLE TEXT

Matthew 6:5-8

CONSIDER

Some have used this passage to suggest that public prayer is inappropriate for Christians. This is not the choice involved in Jesus' instruction. This is not about whether our prayer is public or private; it is about whether our prayer is artificial or genuine. The focus of our Lord here is on teaching us to be honest and careful about our heart when we pray.

There are two things Jesus says must be avoided in genuine prayer. The first is praying to impress others. The second is praying to impress God. The problem with each is that we forget who we are addressing. Jesus is saying prayer needs to be honest and genuine, a true expression of what is in our hearts. He is not condemning public community prayer. It was customary for the Jews to pause in whatever they were doing midday to offer prayers in conjunction with the evening sacrifice in the temple. And "go into your room" (v. 6) should not be taken literally, since many of Jesus' hearers lived in simple homes that lacked such a private room. The point is that prayer must be directed to God alone.

The other matter of Jesus' concern is what he calls "empty phrases" (v. 7). Obviously words don't impress God; a contrite and surrendered heart does. Children have so much to teach us here. We seem to get the idea that in order to let God know how serious we are in prayer, we have to go on and on with many words. I love the faith of children, who, when concerned for someone, simply pray, "Lord, please be with Grandpa," and this is enough for them. Sometimes our wordy prayers do not come from pious faith but from our anxiety over whether or not God will hear us.

Jesus invites us to leave these worries behind and then gives a plain description of how to pray. It is instructive to note that when the disciples longed to know something about the deep prayer life that Jesus obviously knew, he taught them simply and briefly with the model prayer, the Disciples' Prayer or, as we usually call it, the Lord's Prayer—which we will consider tomorrow.

READING

We do not pray to inform God of our wants. Omniscient as he is, he cannot be informed of anything which he knew not before: and he is always willing to relieve them [our needs]. The chief thing wanting is a fit disposition on our part to receive his grace and blessing. Consequently, one great purpose of prayer is to produce such a disposition in us: to exercise our dependence on God; to increase our desire of the things we ask for; to make us so sensible of our wants that we never cease wrestling till we have prevailed for the blessing.

—*John Wesley*[4]

PRAYER

"Jesus, Son of David, have mercy on me!" (Mark 10:47).

DISCIPLINE (RESPONSE)

Many Christians live in fear of being called on to pray in public, such as in a Sunday school class, at a Bible study, or even with their families. Why would this be? Have we perhaps allowed how we appear to others (intelligent, articulate, and spiritual) to become more important to us than what God knows about our hearts? Or have we possibly fallen into the trap of "many words" in our praying? What might the Lord desire to teach us about being in his presence in silence?

BLESSING

May you know the wooing of the Holy Spirit into times of intimate and authentic communion with the Father. May the Lord deliver you from any and all anxieties about prayer and into the joy of peaceful participation in the life of the Father, Son, and Holy Spirit.

❁ Wednesday in the Fifth Week of Lent

BIBLE TEXT
Matthew 6:9-13

CONSIDER

When the disciples of Jesus wanted to know how to pray, Jesus gave them these few words. It is a simple and beautiful prayer. These are clearly the right words for prayer. After all, they were given to us by our Lord and are prayed daily by Christians around the world and through the centuries. We should be reminded, however, that genuine prayer is not simply a matter of getting the words right. It is more a matter of the heart being so open and so honest before God that we can see him, see ourselves, and see God's power to make us true followers of his Son.

The address "Our Father" (v. 9) gives us courage to offer this prayer. These are momentous petitions, but if God is something like a father, then as beloved children perhaps we can risk approaching him this way. This prayer means to change things and reorder things. We pray, "Your kingdom come, your will be done, on earth as it is in heaven" (v. 10). Our natural impulse may be to imagine that God will change things in the world to our liking. The truth is that this prayer is not for getting what we want but for aligning our hearts toward what God wills.

With the very first word it teaches us to pray differently than we would on our own: "*Our* Father." There are no first-person singular pronouns in this prayer. It is all about *us*—"give us," "forgive us," "lead us," and "deliver us." This teaches us that the idea that a person can follow God without the church is untrue. We pray being mindful of those with whom we share the fellowship of the Lord's Table, but this attention to community also reminds us of all Christians everywhere, of that "great . . . crowd of witnesses" (Heb. 12:1). This is why it is so important for us to pray this prayer aloud with the community of faith. We must have an awareness of each other so that we say it together. The fast ones must slow down, and the slower ones must speed up. We are in this together. So let us pray, "*Our* Father . . ."

READING

In the Episcopal order of worship, the priest sometimes introduces the Lord's Prayer with the words, "Now, as our Savior Christ hath taught us, we are bold to say . . ." The word *bold* is worth thinking about. We do well not to pray the prayer lightly. It takes guts to pray it at all. . . .

"Thy will be done" is what we are saying. That is the climax of the first half of the prayer. We are asking God to be God. . . . We are asking God to make manifest the holiness that is now mostly hidden. . . . "Thy kingdom come . . . on earth" is what we are saying. And if that were suddenly to happen, what then? What would stand and what would fall? . . . Which if any of our most precious visions of what God is and of what human beings are would prove to be more or less on the mark and which would turn out to be phony as three-dollar bills? Boldness indeed. To speak those words is to . . . unleash a power that makes atomic power look like a warm breeze.

—*Frederick Buechner*[5]

PRAYER

Father, hallowed be your name.
Your kingdom come.
Give us each day our daily bread,
and forgive us our sins,
 for we ourselves forgive everyone who is indebted to us.
And lead us not into temptation. (Luke 11:2-4)

DISCIPLINE (RESPONSE)

Do you have a regular discipline of praying with others? The power of praying together and of praying the prayers given to us by the Lord and by the church down through the centuries must not be neglected. If this is not your pattern, perhaps the Lord would strengthen you to lead your family and your faith community in prayer.

BLESSING

The LORD bless you and keep you;
the LORD make his face to shine upon you and be gracious to you;
the LORD lift up his countenance upon you and give you peace.
 (Num. 6:24-26)

❂ Thursday in the Fifth Week of Lent

BIBLE TEXT

Matthew 6:14-15

CONSIDER

Just about the time we are thinking that we can get Jesus' version of true discipleship, he throws in something like this and suddenly it seems impossible again. He taught us to pray, "Forgive us our debts, as we also have forgiven our debtors" (v. 12). That's one thing, and perhaps we can deal with it. But then, almost like an afterthought, he goes back into the heart of the model prayer and plunges the issue of forgiveness right into our hearts. "Unless you forgive each other, you will not be forgiven" (see v. 15). Ouch! This is too hard.

If we really believed these words, would there be so much unforgiveness among us? Jesus knew that with a spirit of unforgiveness lurking in our hearts, everything else in this Sermon on the Mount would unravel. None of it would work, none of it would mean anything, if we refused to live in reconciliation and peace with each other. This is the heart of the gospel. Forgiveness is what distinguishes Christianity from all other religions. No one else has the concept that God, out of his great love, freely and gladly forgives those who are separated from him without them somehow having to earn it. No one else has a Savior who dies on a cross to make possible our forgiveness from sin and then is raised from the dead to have the power to deliver that forgiveness to us. This is it; this is everything. If we don't get this, then we don't get anything.

Now of course we believe in forgiveness as a concept. It's the practice of it that becomes a problem. The purpose and goal of forgiveness is reconciliation. Too often, in the church, we say we offer forgiveness to each other, but then the practical strategy is simply to avoid each other and put the relationship to rest. That's not what Jesus has in mind. Forgiveness does not mean that we pretend nothing wrong happened or that we did not get hurt deeply. Forgiveness means that we give up the need or desire to judge another and that we release that work to God. A poignant question may be, "Would I be willing to accept from God only the degree of forgiveness that I have offered to others?" Most of all, we must pray and ask the Lord of mercy to grant us grace for the beautiful work of forgiveness and reconciliation.

READING

"Father, forgive them, for they know not what they do," said the Divine, making excuse for his murderers, not after it was all over, but at the very moment when he was dying by their hands. Then Jesus had forgiven them already. His prayer the Father must have heard, for he and the Son are one. When the Father succeeded in answering his prayer, then his forgiveness in the hearts of the murderers broke out in sorrow, repentance, and faith. Here was a sin dreadful enough surely—but easy for our Lord to forgive. All that excuse for the misled populace! Lord Christ be thanked for that! That was like thee!

—*George MacDonald*[6]

PRAYER

Almighty and everliving God, in your tender love for the human race you sent your Son our Savior Jesus Christ to take upon him our nature, and to suffer death upon the cross, giving us the example of his great humility: Mercifully grant that we may walk in the way of his suffering, and also share in his resurrection; through Jesus Christ our Lord, who lives and reigns with you and the Holy Spirit, one God, for ever and ever. Amen.[7]

DISCIPLINE (RESPONSE)

Is there any place in your life where the spirit of unforgiveness has taken hold and is robbing you of the peace and joy that God desires for you? God helping you, what courageous step of forgiveness and reconciliation do you need to undertake? Whether or not your move toward reconciliation is received is not your concern. Do what God asks you to do, and leave the results to the grace and mercy of God.

BLESSING

May the Lord grant you courage to offer forgiveness, especially to those who may think they have no need of it. Forgive as the Lord has forgiven you. And may the grace and peace of our Lord Jesus be with you.

❂ Friday in the Fifth Week of Lent

BIBLE TEXT

Matthew 6:16-18

CONSIDER

Jesus really did say, *"When* you fast" (vv. 16, 17). We may wish he had said, *"If* you fast." That would make it easier, but there is no mistaking it. He said, *"When* you fast." Evidently Jesus thinks fasting is the normal discipline of a disciple. This is disturbing—if only these verses were missing. Yet there they are, staring us in the face—three short verses—but how they confront us.

It does seem that in a society where the landscape is dotted with fast-food outlets and restaurants of all types, fasting seems rather out of place. We make a sport of eating out, literally. I have seen several restaurants that are built around sports, whether watching games on the screens or playing the games available at the tables. It's not enough anymore to serve food. We are so bored with food that restaurants have to serve up a whole dining experience, or people won't come.

So these words of Jesus sting. Most serious followers of God have embraced the discipline of fasting. The list of biblical persons who fasted reads like a who's who of Scripture: Moses, David, Elijah, Daniel, Paul, and our Lord Jesus, to name only a few. Jesus knew that we are seduced and distracted every day by what this world offers us for happiness, pleasure, and comfort. In a world like this you really don't need God very much. What does it mean to pray "Give us this day our daily bread" (v. 11) when we can simply go to the grocery store and easily buy bread? This is why in a world of plenty and in a culture of excess we desperately need to learn the spiritual discipline of self-denial. It's a way of remembering that we depend on God alone and draw all our strength and resources from him. We fast to enhance our ability to listen to God. We fast to remember our complete dependency on him. We fast to be sustained only by him. And the promise of Jesus is, "Your Father who sees in secret will reward you" (v. 18).

READING

Lord Jesus, I believe that thou art able and willing to deliver me from all the care and unrest and bondage of my Christian life. I believe thou didst die to set me free, not only in the future, but now and here. I believe thou art stronger than Satan, and that thou canst keep me, even me, in my extreme of weakness, from falling into his snares or yielding obedience to his commands. And, Lord, I am going to trust thee to keep me. I have tried keeping myself, and have failed, and failed most grievously. I am absolutely helpless; so now I will trust thee. I will give myself to thee; I keep back no reserves. Body, soul, and spirit, I present myself to thee, a worthless lump of clay, to be made into anything thy love and thy wisdom shall choose.

—*Hannah Whitall Smith*[8]

PRAYER

Gracious Father, whose blessed Son Jesus Christ came down from heaven to be the true bread which gives life to the world: Evermore give us this bread, that he may live in us, and we in him; who lives and reigns with you and the Holy Spirit, one God, now and for ever. Amen.[9]

DISCIPLINE (RESPONSE)

This is a good point in the Lenten season to assess our spiritual disciplines. Did we commit to fasting at the beginning that has now been forgotten? Now would be a good time to renew the commitment to fast. Perhaps we have been afraid to declare a fast for such a long period. The next two weeks as we move toward Easter may be a time to embrace some kind of fast that could sharpen our spiritual senses and awaken us to things of the Spirit.

BLESSING

May the Lord grant you the strength to embrace self-denial and prayer. Do not be afraid, but trust in the Lord, who desires to assist you. May your hunger for God become sharper than all other hunger pangs until you learn to become satisfied by the very Bread of Heaven. And may the peace of Christ be with you.

❇ Saturday in the Fifth Week of Lent

BIBLE TEXT
Matthew 6:19-34

CONSIDER

We hear in this section of the Sermon on the Mount another significant mark of a true disciple of Jesus Christ. True disciples have their priorities straight. Real disciples know that you simply cannot serve both God and money. That is easy to say but much more difficult to live out in a world like ours. Jesus places the issue on two simple principles.

First, straight priorities are fundamentally a matter of the heart. This is the essence of the entire Sermon on the Mount message. Jesus-style discipleship is an inward reality that results in an outward lifestyle. This seems to be the point of the somewhat strange saying about the eyes that Jesus drops right into the middle of all this. Being persons of light is a matter of how we see. When it comes to possessions and all that this world pretends to offer, do we see clearly? Or do we get blinded by the glitter of it all and suddenly find ourselves enmeshed in the values and priorities of this world?

Second, having straight priorities is a matter of exercising discipline in our choices. Choices such as, "How will I spend the 168 hours available to me every week?" Choices such as, "What will I do when the company offers me a promotion, but it will mean more time away from home?" Making these choices well requires that our values and priorities are aligned with the values and priorities of the kingdom of God rather than with those of this world.

Maybe that's why we are sometimes offended when Jesus starts talking like this, because he calls us to a completely different way. He says to us, "Kingdom people are not even concerned with the same things the world is concerned with. Kingdom people give themselves to other things, other priorities that move them in a totally different direction." Worship and worry do not get along well in the same heart. They fight against each other. So the simple word of Jesus to us is, "Do not worry." Now many may say, "Sure, that is easy to say, but how does one really avoid worry in a world like ours?" What if we put it in the same terms that

Jesus did? It is a choice. It's as simple as that, really—we have a choice. Jesus makes it clear throughout his life and teaching that the alternative to anxiety over what we do not control is to release our grasp of what we do control. That attitude of release is what he is calling us to here.

READING

Most of us are pagans in a crisis. We think and act like pagans; only one out of a hundred is daring enough to bank his faith in the character of God.

The golden rule for understanding in spiritual matters is not intellect, but obedience. Discernment in the spiritual world is never gained by intellect; in the common-sense world it is. If a man wants scientific knowledge, intellectual curiosity is his guide; but if he wants insight into what Jesus Christ teaches, he can only get it by obedience. If things are dark to us spiritually, it is because there is something we will not do. Intellectual darkness comes because of ignorance; spiritual darkness comes because of something I do not intend to obey.

—Oswald Chambers[10]

PRAYER

Almighty God, who by your holy apostle has taught us to set our affection on things above: Grant us so to labor in this life that we may ever be mindful of our citizenship in those heavenly places where our Savior Christ has gone before; who lives and reigns with you and the Holy Spirit, ever one God, world without end. Amen.[11]

DISCIPLINE (RESPONSE)

What would it take to eliminate worry from your life? Hint: the answer is not more money and more time; the answer is to align your thinking and practices with the values of God's kingdom. What initial steps toward that alignment could you take in the next few weeks?

BLESSING

May the Lord grant you wisdom to make good decisions. May the grace of God free you *from* enslavement to the priorities of this world and free you *to* the values of his kingdom. And may the peace of Christ rule and reign in your heart.

* The Sixth Week of Lent
(Fifth Sunday to Day 34)

◉ Fifth Sunday in Lent

BIBLE TEXT

Matthew 7:1-6

CONSIDER

A man was visiting his five-year-old neighbor, Andrew, one day. They were talking about his new class at school. Suddenly Andrew ran over to the shelf and pulled down his kindergarten class photo to share with his friend and neighbor. He began to describe each classmate.

"This is Robert. He hits everyone. This is Stephen. He never listens to the teacher. This is Mark. He chases us and is very noisy." He had a comment like that about every person in his class. Finally he came to his own image. Andrew pointed to his own picture and said, "And this is me. I'm just sitting here minding my own business."

Isn't it amazing how early we learn to put ourselves in the very best light? Jesus knows this about us. He knows how hard we work at self-protection and self-justification. And he knows that in order to make ourselves look better or just to feel better we become experts in criticism. So Jesus comes along in this pesky Sermon on the Mount and says, "Listen, friends, if you really want to be like me, then quit being so hard on each other. Exercise some of the same mercy that God exercises toward you every day." Jesus uses a comic illustration of a speck and a log to get us to see that we have no business pointing out the faults and shortcomings of others until we have taken a good, long, and honest look at our own shortcomings.

If we take Jesus' words seriously here, then we do not have the luxury of allowing our words of anger or frustration to fly. It's not good enough for us to think, "Well, I was just frustrated; it's nothing personal" or "I'm just a truth teller; I don't mean any harm by it." According to Jesus we don't have that luxury. The principle of sowing and reaping is in effect, so we need to be really careful about our attitude when evaluating someone else.

This word of Jesus is linked to the fifth beatitude back in Matthew 5: "Blessed are the merciful, for they shall receive mercy" (v. 7). If we really understood God's preference for mercy, we would not be nearly so quick to judge others. In fact, if we really took Jesus' words to heart, if we ever found ourselves in a place of speaking judgment or correction, it would come with tears.

READING

The repetition of **brother** in verses 3-5 suggests Christ is concerned with a condemning spirit in the Christian community. Jesus does not mean that His followers never analyze the behavior or attitude of others. Rather, His followers are to first judge their own behavior and attitude.

When one's own behavior or attitude has been corrected, a person is better able to analyze another's. One is also more inclined to show mercy after dealing with the reality of one's own faults. John Wesley comments that one should not judge a brother "without full, clear, certain knowledge, without absolute necessity, without tender love."

—*Roger Hahn*[1]

PRAYER

O Blessed Lord, I beseech Thee to pour down upon me such grace as may not only cleanse this life of mine, but beautify it a little, if it be Thy will,—before I go hence and am no more seen. Grant that I may love Thee with all my heart and soul and mind and strength, and my neighbor as myself—and that I may persevere unto the end; through Jesus Christ—Amen.[2]

DISCIPLINE (RESPONSE)

Sometimes the Lord places before us the necessity of speaking a word of correction to a brother or sister in Christ. If you are sensing the direction of the Spirit to do this, check your heart by the help of the Holy Spirit. What is your motive? How is the tenderness of your spirit toward this person? What will it mean to be merciful to him or her as the Lord has been merciful to you?

BLESSING

May you go into this new week as a vessel of God's love and mercy. May God help you to know the condition of your heart before you speak a correcting word to anyone. And may the grace and peace of our Lord Jesus abide with you.

❂ Monday in the Sixth Week of Lent

BIBLE TEXT

Matthew 7:7-11

CONSIDER

What are we to make of the fact that after calling us to this amazing life of grace, forgiveness, and righteousness, after nearly three chapters of the loftiest kind of vision of what it means to be a true disciple, Jesus now stops, looks at us, and says, "You want it? Just ask, and you will receive. Do you desire to live a life that is totally acceptable to God? Just seek it, and you will find it. Would you like to be pleasing to the Father? Just knock, and it will be opened up to you."

Really? Could this be true? Will God actually give us everything we need to live the kind of life that his holiness demands? Jesus knows that the world in which we live regularly pulls the rug out from under our feet so that we are wary to trust anyone. So he gives a simple illustration to help us see how God wants to treat us. It's like a father and his son. If the son asks his father for bread, would the father give him a stone instead? Of course not, that's ridiculous. If the son asks for a fish, will the father give him a snake? No, that would be child abuse. But it seems that this is really our fear when we hear Jesus offer us everything we need to live out the demands of the Sermon on the Mount.

Jesus is simply saying that the life of a genuine disciple is available for the asking, but we have to trust the character of the Giver. We have to trust that what he gives really is the best and really is what we need. Jesus is offering a relationship of total trust, like a young child trusting his or her father. Have you ever watched a young child leap from a ledge into his or her father's arms? This is a picture of the relationship of trust God desires with us. Jesus' point is simple: if you earthly fathers can understand what it means to want to give the very best to your children, how much more does your heavenly Father want to give good gifts to you?

READING

And, first, all who desire the grace of God are to wait for it in the way of prayer. This is the express direction of our Lord himself. . . . Here we are in the plainest manner directed to ask, in order to, or as a means of, receiving; to seek, in order to find, the grace of God, the pearl of great price; and to knock, to continue asking and seeking, if we would enter into his kingdom.

. . . That no doubt might remain, our Lord labours this point in a more peculiar manner. He appeals to every man's own heart: "What man is there of you, who, if his son ask bread, will he give him a stone? Or, if he ask a fish, will he give him a serpent? If ye then, being evil, know how to give good gifts unto your children," . . . "How much more shall your heavenly Father give the Holy Spirit to them that ask him?"

—*John Wesley*[3]

PRAYER

O merciful Creator, whose hand is open wide to satisfy the needs of every living creature: Make us, we beseech thee, ever thankful for thy loving providence; and grant that we, remembering the account that we must one day give, may be faithful stewards of thy bounty; through Jesus Christ our Lord, who with thee and the Holy Spirit liveth and reigneth, one God, for ever and ever. Amen.[4]

DISCIPLINE (RESPONSE)

There is plenty of evidence in your life to discern how much you are trusting God as the Provider of your needs. How is your trust? What steps could you take even this week to lean more on God's gracious provision and less on your own ability to secure your life?

BLESSING

May you so trust the Giver that you are able to leap into his waiting arms as a child leaps into the arms of a father. Bring your needs to the Father and trust him to care for you. And may the peace of Christ keep you from worry and fear.

◉ Tuesday in the Sixth Week of Lent

BIBLE TEXT
Matthew 7:12

CONSIDER

This well-known verse is something of a watershed in the Sermon on the Mount. This is no isolated instruction, disconnected from all that has gone before. It is summative; it encapsulates the spirit of what Jesus has been teaching throughout. Jesus' observation that living by the so-called Golden Rule sums up the "Law and the Prophets" takes us all the way back to Matthew 5:17 and marks out the beginning and the ending of the heart of his teaching in this sermon. Treating others in the way that we ourselves would want to be treated is in one sense a simple, nearly child-like instruction. And yet, according to Jesus, it sums up everything that he has been teaching from 5:17 up to this point.

Although this Golden Rule is well known and widely quoted by people throughout society, it is really only in the kingdom of God that this rule of life could be fully lived and known. The reason for this is because the ability to live in this way does not rise naturally from within us. To live in this way is a work of God's grace that can only be fully realized in us when we surrender fully to the lordship of Jesus Christ. It is only by living out this Golden Rule under the lordship of Jesus that we are prevented from making it into a tool of manipulation. We do not treat people this way only so that we might receive back from them what we want. We are being called to treat others the way we would like to be treated, not *so* we will be treated well in return, but *regardless* of how we are treated in return. This way of living is the right thing to do no matter how others may treat us in response.

This rule makes practical the central ethic to which Jesus calls us: to "love the Lord your God with all your heart and with all your soul and with all your mind" (22:37), which must lead us to "love your neighbor as yourself" (v. 39). As such, this rule is not only about shaping our actions in particular ways that move us toward compassion and kindness but also about shaping our hearts in ways that cause us truly to become as salt and light in the world.

READING

Jesus Christ came to make the great laws of God incarnate in human life; that is the miracle of God's grace. We are to be written epistles, "known and read of all men." There is no allowance whatever in the New Testament for the man who says he is saved by grace but who does not produce the graceful goods. Jesus Christ by His Redemption can make our actual life in keeping with our religious profession.

In our study of the Sermon on the Mount it would be like a baptism of light to allow the principles of Jesus Christ to soak right down into our very makeup. His statements are not put up as standards for us to attain; God remakes us, puts His Holy Spirit in us, then the Holy Spirit applies the principles to us and enables us to work them out by His guidance.

—Oswald Chambers[5]

PRAYER

Take thou the full possession of my heart; raise there thy throne, and command there as thou dost in heaven. Being created by thee, let me live to thee; being created for thee, let me ever act for thy glory; being redeemed by thee, let me render unto thee what is thine, and let my spirit ever cleave to thee alone. Amen.[6]

DISCIPLINE (RESPONSE)

Reflecting on the past several days, would others say of you that the Golden Rule finds expression in your life—your words, actions, and attitudes? Where there may be any sense of uncertainty in this, ask the Lord to sharpen your mind so that in each encounter of this day and the days to come you will be keenly aware not only of treating others as you would be treated but also of treating others as Jesus would treat them.

BLESSING

The Lord bless you and keep you through this day. May the Lord allow his perfect love to flow through you to everyone you meet. May the rule of love be the rule of your living today. And may the peace of Christ reign in your heart.

❁ Wednesday in the Sixth Week of Lent

BIBLE TEXT

Matthew 7:13-20

CONSIDER

The only way to live what Jesus is teaching is to surrender all of life to his lordship. Some have understood the narrow road admonition as a call to effort and discipline. In one sense this is true, but walking the narrow road of Jesus-style life is not really about our tenacious ability. This narrow-road journey is about taking the path of grace instead of self-effort. It's about trusting God to remake us from the inside out; it is not about trying to remake ourselves from the outside in. Jesus has a warning for us as we come near the end of this Sermon on the Mount. His warning could be summarized as, "Be careful because you *can* fake it. It *is* possible to look like a Christian and yet not have an authentic relationship with Christ."

The warning really comes on two fronts. One is to be careful of spiritual leaders who are faking it, because of the tremendous damage they can do. The second is to be careful that we are not counted among them, because it is possible to fake it—at least for a while. Jesus says, "Beware of false prophets" (v. 15). Israel was familiar with false prophets. False prophets in Israel led the people to believe that their halfhearted discipleship was okay. That message is still around today. False prophets today would lead folks to believe that God really isn't all that serious about sin or judgment. "Just do your best," they say, "and everything will be okay." Their words sound full of grace and mercy, but in reality they lead to destruction. God demands more than our best shot. God demands our holiness.

A true disciple of Jesus will consistently, quietly, and faithfully produce the fruit of a Jesus-style life. Is there evidence in your life of authentic discipleship? Or are you going through life trying to tie imitation fruit on your branches? Genuine fruit includes not only Christlike character, such as the list in Galatians 5, but also the fruit of ministry. The only way to be assured of good fruit is to embrace what Jesus said in John's gospel.

"Abide in me, and I in you. As the branch cannot bear fruit by itself, unless it abides in the vine, neither can you, unless you abide in me" (15:4).

READING

We are the agents of the Creative Spirit in this world. Real advance in the spiritual life, then, means accepting this vocation with all it involves. Not merely turning over the pages of an engineering magazine and enjoying the pictures, but putting on overalls and getting on with the job. The real spiritual life must be horizontal as well as vertical; spread more and more as well as aspire more and more.

—*Evelyn Underhill*[7]

PRAYER

Lord of mercy, we confess that only by your grace can we find the strength and courage to live as your children in this broken world. Grant us, in your love, all that we need to bear witness to your redeeming love. Give us eyes to see and ears to hear the true needs around us; and grant us the willingness to serve as you would serve. Amen.

DISCIPLINE (RESPONSE)

Does the fruit of your discipleship make it evident that you are an authentic follower of Jesus Christ? What specifically would you point to in your life as evidence of unqualified obedience to Christ?

BLESSING

God bless you today to bear the fruit of righteousness that is the life of Jesus shining through you. May you use the grace of God to walk faithfully the narrow road of life as a servant of Christ and a servant to all. And may the peace of our Lord be with you.

❂ Thursday in the Sixth Week of Lent

BIBLE TEXT

Matthew 7:21-23

CONSIDER

These may be some of the most important words of the Sermon on the Mount. Jesus seems to reach back to the statement in 5:20, when he said, "Unless your righteousness exceeds that of the scribes and Pharisees, you will never enter the kingdom of heaven." The righteousness that Jesus is looking for in his disciples is much more than simply having an intellectual command of his teachings. His words must go down deep into our hearts and create a way of living that is the natural outflow of a life that belongs entirely to him.

There is a penetrating and personal question at this point. Have we so allowed the Spirit of Jesus to take over our lives that rather than just standing on the very edge of holiness hoping we are good enough, we've been changed at the very core of our beings? Is "follower of Jesus" simply one more descriptor in our multifaceted lives? Or is being a follower of Jesus the essence of our identity? Is being a Christian more than something we try to do? Is it who we are? This is what Jesus wants to know. Grace has not come so we can live however we want. Grace has come so we can be holy and pure and truly righteous. Do you know what happens when we seek to live in righteousness like that? When we take holiness with great seriousness, we soon find out how unable we are to be faithful on our own. We are driven back into the arms of a merciful and gracious God.

It's only as we take seriously the call of God to be holy that we can fully experience the grace of God that gives the power to live a holy life. This is when the gospel truly becomes good news, because there we can see that Jesus has done and is doing for us what we cannot do for ourselves. Thanks be to God! He is all our righteousness; we stand complete in him and worship him. It is from this place of holy love filling our hearts that we have the capacity to do the will of God in a way that makes us recognizable to the Lord.

READING

The Holy Spirit is the One who brings the appearance and the reality into one in us; He does *in* us what Jesus did *for* us. The mighty redemption of God is made actual in our experience by the living efficacy of the Holy Ghost. The New Testament never asks us to *believe* the Holy Spirit; it asks us to *receive* Him. He makes the appearance and the reality one and the same thing. He *works in* our salvation, and we have to *work it out*, with fear and trembling lest we forget to.

—*Oswald Chambers*[8]

PRAYER

O God, Author of eternal light, do Thou shed forth continual day upon us who watch for Thee; that our lips may praise Thee, our life may bless Thee, our meditations may glorify Thee; through Christ our Lord—Amen.[9]

DISCIPLINE (RESPONSE)

How deep and wide is your faith? Does your following of Jesus get involved in every corner of your life? Is your every thought and every action shaped by the life of Christ in you? Check your heart today, by the help of the Holy Spirit. Does your Christian life pass the test of authenticity?

BLESSING

The LORD will keep you from all evil;
    he will keep your life.
The LORD will keep
    your going out and your coming in
    from this time forth and forevermore. (Ps. 121:7-8)

❁ Friday in the Sixth Week of Lent

BIBLE TEXT
Matthew 7:24-27

CONSIDER

This closing saying of the Sermon on the Mount connects to yesterday's text. The idea is simple: it is possible for us to go through life and have all the Christian externals down, but there is coming a day, the storm day, when the real substance of what we are is revealed.

We should note that Jesus' story does not intend to contrast good construction practices with bad construction practices. The houses both look good and substantial. His warning here has to do with an incredibly foolish decision made by one of the builders about the choice of a site. One of them made the unbelievable choice to build in a dry riverbed. Such dry riverbeds exist in the southwest United States. It's kind of amazing to go over a bridge with a sign attached to it saying "So-and-So River," but there's not a drop of water to be found. So it's imaginable that someone might be enticed to use that land for a building site. It's nice and flat, easily accessible, and seems like a good place to put down a foundation. However, I have seen what happens to those dry riverbeds when a hard rain comes. In a second they become raging torrents, sweeping away everything in their paths.

The foolish man here chose the easy site without considering the potential consequences of his choice. Jesus simply says this is the one who seems to have it all together on the outside, but it doesn't go deep; it's not on the right foundation.

The lesson is intended to hit home. If you are really honest about your discipleship, is it more talk or more substance? Do you know how to do and say all the right things, but the character of Jesus hasn't really gone deeply into your heart? You may have a good spiritual house, but Jesus just wants to know, "Rock or sand? Talk or action? Outside or inside?"

Authentic discipleship pays the price of building on the rock. Where are you building and why are you building? What have you really bought into as one who professes to be a Christ follower? A system and tradition? Or life in the Jesus way? The houses may look just the same for a very long time. But one day, the foundation will be revealed.

READING

I am . . . to show the wisdom of him that doeth [the Lord's sayings], that buildeth his house upon a rock. He indeed is wise, "who doeth the will of my Father which is in heaven." He is truly wise, whose "righteousness exceeds the righteousness of the Scribes and Pharisees." He is poor in spirit; knowing himself even as also he is known. He sees and feels all his sin, and all his guilt, till it is washed away by the atoning blood. He is conscious of his lost estate, of the wrath of God abiding on him, and of his utter inability to help himself, till he is filled with peace and joy in the Holy Ghost. He is meek and gentle, patient toward all men, never "returning evil for evil, or railing for railing, but contrariwise blessing," till he overcomes evil with good. His soul is athirst for nothing on earth, but only for God, the living God. . . . He loves the Lord his God with all his heart, and with all his mind, and soul, and strength. He alone shall enter into the kingdom of heaven, who, in this spirit, doeth good unto all men.

—*John Wesley*[10]

PRAYER

O Lord, with whom are Strength and Wisdom, put forth Thy strength, I implore Thee, for Thine own sake and for our sakes, and stand up to help us; for we are deceivable and weak persons, frail and brief, unstable and afraid, unless Thou put the might of Thy Holy Spirit within us—Amen, O Lord—Amen.[11]

DISCIPLINE (RESPONSE)

Are you building on the rock that is not only faith in Jesus but also daily life lived in his name and after his pattern? What goals could you set that would help you to strengthen the foundation of your Christian life?

BLESSING

Now to him who is able to keep you from stumbling and to present you blameless before the presence of his glory with great joy, to the only God, our Savior, through Jesus Christ our Lord, be glory, majesty, dominion, and authority, before all time and now and forever. Amen. (Jude vv. 24-25)

❀ Saturday in the Sixth Week of Lent

BIBLE TEXT
Matthew 7:28-29

CONSIDER

Many years ago, having committed to memory the entire Sermon on the Mount, I stood before my congregation one Sunday evening and simply recited it. I was extremely nervous about doing so because I was unsure of how the people would respond to a simple recitation of these Bible verses. That night as I concluded with these words of the final two verses and said "Amen," I was aware that something significant had happened in the hearts of those gathered. I believe we experienced anew what the first hearers of Jesus' sermon experienced. The amazement was not simply about the truth of these statements. It was more about a deep awareness of the spiritual authority of our Lord himself that remains in the reading, hearing, and reflection upon these words. We sense that these are more than good ideas or pithy sayings upon which to construct our discipleship. These are indeed the words of life because they reveal the very heart of God and his passion for us as his children. As Douglas Hare writes, "We are meant to hear in it not merely a wise teacher but our Lord and King."[12]

READING

This summing up is a descriptive note by the Holy Spirit of the way in which the people who heard Jesus Christ were impressed by His doctrine. Its application for us is not, "What would Jesus do?" but, "What did Jesus *say*?" As we concentrate on what He said, we can stake our immortal souls upon His words. It is a question of scriptural concentration, not of sentimental consecration. When Jesus brings something home by His word, don't shirk it. . . . The Holy Spirit's voice is as gentle as a zephyr, the merest check; when you hear it, do you say, "But that is only a tiny detail; the Holy Spirit cannot mean that; it is much too trivial a thing"? The Holy Spirit does mean that, and at the risk of being thought fanatical you must obey.

—*Oswald Chambers*[13]

PRAYER

Almighty God, who hast caused the light of eternal life to shine upon the world, we beseech Thee that our hearts may be so kindled with heavenly desires, and Thy love so shed abroad in us by Thy Holy Spirit, that we may continually seek the things which are above; and, abiding in purity of heart and mind, may at length attain unto Thine everlasting kingdom, there to dwell in the glorious light of Thy presence, world without end—Amen.[14]

DISCIPLINE (RESPONSE)

Spend several moments in silence today, meditating upon the whole of what Jesus has taught us through the Sermon on the Mount. Let the Holy Spirit impress upon your heart a fresh word of challenge and hope that will guide you through the remembrance of the passion, death, and resurrection of our Lord, that it may truly change you "from one degree of glory to another" (2 Cor. 3:18).

BLESSING

Now may the God of peace who brought again from the dead our Lord Jesus, the great shepherd of the sheep, by the blood of the eternal covenant, equip you with everything good that you may do his will, working in us that which is pleasing in his sight, through Jesus Christ, to whom be glory forever and ever. Amen. (Heb. 13:20-21)

* Holy Week
(Passion/Palm Sunday to Day 40)

The devotions for Holy Week are intentionally shorter and simpler. During this week we especially need the space for quiet reflection and prayer. Spend the larger part of your devotional time during these days slowly and quietly thinking upon and praying over the love of God that is so profoundly demonstrated in the passion of our Lord.

⚙ Passion/Palm Sunday

BIBLE TEXT

Matthew 21:1-11

CONSIDER

Jesus was generally acclaimed by the crowds as the Hero-Miracle Worker. He could heal, cast out demons, and make bread for crowds. So when he came into Jerusalem, his public approval rating was off the charts. Word got out that he was coming into the city, so the crowds went out from Jerusalem toward Bethphage with palm branches heralding the arrival, of whom? The Hero. The Miracle Worker. The Messiah who would grant them all their wishes. Jesus was doing, they thought, exactly what they had always wanted him to do. He was riding into the city as a king to proclaim his rule and reign. Perhaps they didn't notice that Jesus wasn't riding a white stallion, the sign of a conquering warrior. He was on a donkey, a symbol of peace. He wasn't coming to overthrow the government or the religious system per se. He knew, and apparently was the only one who really knew, that he was headed for a cross.

In just a short time we will gather to celebrate Easter, proclaiming the glory of our risen Lord. We will sing praises to the Savior, who won the victory and now sits at the right hand of God in glory. It's the picture of Jesus we love best. But when we celebrate the victory of Jesus, will we really know what we are cheering about? Will we just be joining the crowd and getting caught up in the emotion of it all? Or will we be able to celebrate with tears of joy because we have been to Golgotha and realized that he died there for the love of you and me?

PRAYER FOR PALM SUNDAY

Almighty and everliving God, in your tender love for the human race you sent your Son our Savior Jesus Christ to take upon him our nature, and to suffer death upon the cross, giving us the example of his great humility: Mercifully grant that we may walk in the way of his suffering, and also share in his resurrection; through Jesus Christ our Lord.[1] Amen.

❀ Monday in Holy Week

BIBLE TEXT
John 12:1-11

CONSIDER

This passage is essentially about worship. Two ways of approaching Jesus are contrasted here. One is very sensible; the other makes almost no sense.

Martha, in characteristic fashion, is busy serving. Don't be too quick to fault her for that; it is her worship. Mary is a bit different. She sees things others don't see, and she worships in a surprising way. It's "six days before the Passover" (v. 1), which means the cross is coming, and Mary seems to understand.

So without a word Mary breaks the neck off a jar of expensive perfume and pours out the precious contents on the feet of Jesus. Suddenly the room grows deathly quiet, and all eyes are on Jesus and Mary. He doesn't say a word. He simply watches as this grateful woman, with tears running down her cheeks, washes his feet with this oil and wipes them off with her hair. It was a beautiful moment. Then Judas opens his mouth. Before we rush to judge Judas, perhaps we should consider the possibility that Judas speaks for all of us. He has the sensible idea: give the money to the poor.

Many of us love to be sensible and practical people. That is not a bad thing, but would we ever dare to be extravagant in our worship? Would we ever dare to show our love for Jesus in a way that wasn't sensible? The point is that we, like Judas, can become so caught up on the practical and sensible that we risk losing sight of what it really means to worship the Lord in complete surrender and love.

PRAYER FOR HOLY MONDAY

Almighty God, whose dear Son went not up to joy but first he suffered pain, and entered not into glory before he was crucified: Mercifully grant that we, walking in the way of the cross, may find it none other than the way of life and peace; through Jesus Christ your Son our Lord.[2] Amen.

❂ Tuesday in Holy Week

BIBLE TEXT
John 12:20-36

CONSIDER
The gospel lesson for today opens with the account of some people who just wanted to see Jesus. We understand that what they were asking for was an opportunity to visit with him. This is a very simple request, right? But do you notice that Jesus really never answered their question? He responded by talking about his destiny of laying down his life.

Throughout his ministry, Jesus has tried to proclaim the coming of God's kingdom to his people, the Jews. For the most part, they would not listen. So just before Jesus goes to the cross, here come these Greeks with a simple question. Can we see Jesus? Could it be that these Greeks represent all of us who are Gentiles? Perhaps their question is our question: "Can we see Jesus? Is the promise of the kingdom for us too?"

The answer is yes; they can see Jesus. But they will see him as the suffering Savior, lifted up on a cross: "I, when I am lifted up from the earth, will draw all people to myself" (v. 32). This is how you ruin a good religion. You ruin it by bringing up that cross stuff all the time. So often the Jesus we really want to see is the one who makes life simple and enjoyable. After all, why does life have to be so hard? Our religion doesn't have to be complicated; it's supposed to be simple, right?

Is your religion simple? Is it nonthreatening and comfortable? Do you ever shudder when in the shadow of the cross you come face-to-face with your *undoneness* before God? If not, then you still haven't seen Jesus. All this talk about the cross may ruin a good religion, but it is through the cross that our sins have been forgiven and we have eternal life.

PRAYER FOR HOLY TUESDAY
O God, by the passion of your blessed Son you made an instrument of shameful death to be for us the means of life: Grant us so to glory in the cross of Christ, that we may gladly suffer shame and loss for the sake of your Son our Savior Jesus Christ.[3] Amen.

✸ Wednesday in Holy Week

BIBLE TEXT
John 13:21-32

CONSIDER

We see in the Bible how the early church came to tell the story of Judas. It's easy to write Judas off as a bad guy. However, here is one who was chosen by the Son of God to be among the Twelve. He was taught and then sent to minister with authority. So what happened?

Perhaps our inability to really answer the question is why the story of Judas bothers us so much. The truth is, every one of us is capable of doing what Judas did. If you think you're not, you are in a very dangerous spiritual condition. Even the other eleven disciples, though they judged Judas, revealed their own uncertainly about it at the Last Supper. When Jesus said, "One of you will betray me" (v. 21), they all asked the question, "Is it I?" (Matt. 26:22; Mark 14:19). Evidently they knew that the capacity for betrayal was in them.

And it is in us. That's why we need to be careful that we don't too quickly categorize Judas as the bad guy and write him off. He walked a path that we could easily walk. Worse than his betrayal, however, is the collapse of his faith in the God of grace. Professor Ray Anderson tells the story of seeing across the top of the mirror of a public restroom in block letters made with a blue felt-tip the words "Judas come home—all is forgiven!" He thought about whom the message was for—a prodigal son, perhaps. He thought about who had left the message—maybe a grieving father.[4] Could it be that you have looked deep into your own soul and discovered Judas possibilities? Come to the Christ, who in the midst of your failure is willing to forgive, heal, and make you new.

PRAYER FOR HOLY WEDNESDAY

Lord God, whose blessed Son our Savior gave his body to be whipped and his face to be spit upon: Give us grace to accept joyfully the sufferings of the present time, confident of the glory that shall be revealed; through Jesus Christ your Son our Lord.[5] Amen.

❁ Maundy Thursday

BIBLE TEXT

1 Corinthians 11:23-26

CONSIDER

You can see it at the funeral of a Christian: the pain of loss and yet the joy of home going. Several experiences in our lives can be like this, joy and pain somehow all mixed up into one emotion-laden experience. When we come to the Lord's Table, which is it? Is it a celebration of joy or a remembrance of suffering? Many have said that in their experience of worship, Communion has often felt more like a funeral service.

Recently in our tradition, however, we have been recovering the idea that Communion is Eucharist, a great thanksgiving. It's a time of joy and celebration because the provision of the cross has come to us through the glorious reality of resurrection. As Dr. Rob Staples has written, "The Lord's Supper is a *fiesta*, not a funeral."[6] True enough. We are celebrating our true victory through Jesus Christ.

But Communion is also an identification with the suffering and death of our Lord. Participating in his victory does not mean we are excluded from his suffering. Paul expresses it so well: "that I may know him and the power of his resurrection, and may share his sufferings, becoming like him in his death" (Phil. 3:10). It's really easy to like that first part, the resurrection part, but we may bristle at the second part, the suffering part. We like the joy; we don't like the pain.

Communion is indeed a time of celebration, a feast of grace. But in our desire to experience the joy and fellowship of the sacrament, we must not avoid its more threatening and challenging implications.

PRAYER FOR MAUNDY THURSDAY

Almighty Father, whose dear Son, on the night before he suffered, instituted the Sacrament of his Body and Blood: Mercifully grant that we may receive it thankfully in remembrance of Jesus Christ our Lord, who in these holy mysteries gives us a pledge of eternal life; and who now lives and reigns with you and the Holy Spirit, one God, for ever and ever. Amen.[7]

✸ Good Friday

BIBLE TEXT
Isaiah 53:1-6

CONSIDER

In the 1998 film *Saving Private Ryan*, just before the soldiers who were sent to bring Private Ryan to safety are able to deliver him, they are enmeshed in a terrible battle. All of them are killed. But just before the captain dies, he grabs Ryan by the jacket and whispers with his last breath, "Earn this."[8] It haunts James Ryan for the rest of his life. The film ends with the sixty-five-year-old Ryan visiting the graves in Normandy of the men who saved his life. He is overcome with emotion. In that moment he looks hopefully into the eyes of his wife and pleads, "Tell me I have led a good life. . . . Tell me I'm a good man."[9]

When someone dies for us, it demands a response. Certainly our response on this holy day should include expressions of gratitude to God. However, expressing our gratitude needs to go far beyond an emotional response to the image of Jesus on the cross. Gratitude should also issue in a way of life that is a response to the reason our Lord gave himself for us. Jesus died to free us from enslavement to sin and death. Jesus defeated sin and death by his death and resurrection. Thus we are able, by the grace and mercy of God, to live our lives in freedom from sin and in the sure hope of the resurrection. If we are walking through life with a sense of defeat and hopelessness, we are missing the good news of the gospel. Our Good Friday opportunity is not only to recognize the depth of our sin that was answered on the cross but also to embrace lives that are marked by freedom from the world's values and illumined by the bright hope for the redemption of all things in Christ.

PRAYER FOR GOOD FRIDAY

Almighty God, we pray you graciously to behold this your family, for whom our Lord Jesus Christ was willing to be betrayed, and given into the hands of sinners, and to suffer death upon the cross; who now lives and reigns with you and the Holy Spirit, one God, for ever and ever. Amen.[10]

❂ Holy Saturday

BIBLE TEXT
John 19:38-42

CONSIDER

Were you there when they crucified my Lord?
Were you there when they crucified my Lord?
O sometimes it causes me to tremble, tremble, tremble!
Were you there when they crucified my Lord?

Were you there when they nailed Him to a tree?
Were you there when they nailed Him to a tree?
O sometimes it causes me to tremble, tremble, tremble!
Were you there when they nailed Him to a tree?

Were you there when they laid Him in a tomb?
Were you there when they laid Him in a tomb?
O sometimes it causes me to tremble, tremble, tremble!
Were you there when they laid Him in a tomb?[11]

PRAYER FOR HOLY SATURDAY

O God, Creator of heaven and earth: Grant that, as the crucified body of your dear Son was laid in the tomb and rested on this holy Sabbath, so we may await with him the coming of the third day, and rise with him to newness of life; who now lives and reigns with you and the Holy Spirit, one God, for ever and ever. Amen.[12]

✳ Easter Day

We come now to the culmination of the Lenten journey: the celebration of the resurrection of our Lord Jesus Christ. This is everything, the center of our faith. We are a resurrection people. Resurrection is not a one-time event that happened only to Jesus. Resurrection is the transforming power and ultimate hope that was unleashed in the world through the obedience of Christ and the power of God. The power of resurrection now impacts everyone who confesses, "Jesus Christ is Lord." The power of resurrection is not only for individual Christians but especially for the people of God who are gathered by the Spirit and sent into the world as the body of Christ. Our task as the church of Jesus Christ is to live together and in this world as an authentic expression of the in-breaking kingdom of God. We announce with our words and by our transformed lives:

Alleluia. Christ is risen.
The Lord is risen indeed. Alleluia.[1]

BIBLE TEXT
John 20:1-18

PRAYER FOR EASTER DAY

Almighty God, who through your only-begotten Son Jesus Christ overcame death and opened to us the gate of everlasting life: Grant that we, who celebrate with joy the day of the Lord's resurrection, may be raised from the death of sin by your life-giving Spirit; through Jesus Christ our Lord, who lives and reigns with you and the Holy Spirit, one God, now and for ever. Amen.[2]

* Notes

PAGE 3

1. Claudia F. Hernaman, "Lord, Who throughout These Forty Days" (1873), *Hymnary.org*, http://www.hymnary.org/text/lord_who_throughout_these_forty_days.

THE BEGINNING OF LENT

1. Brennan Manning, *The Signature of Jesus: The Call to a Life Marked by Holy Passion and Relentless Faith* (Colorado Springs: Multnomah Books, 1992), 128.

2. John Heagle, *On the Way* (Chicago: Thomas More Press, 1981), 210, quoted in Manning, *The Signature of Jesus*, 128.

3. Bobby Gross, *Living the Christian Year: Time to Inhabit the Story of God* (Downers Grove, IL: InterVarsity Press, 2009), 141.

4. Matthew Henry, *Concise Commentary on the Whole Bible* (1706; repr., Christ Notes), comment on Isa. 58:3-12, http://www.christnotes.org/commentary .php?com=mhc&b=23&c=58.

5. Prayer by John Henry Newman, in Mary Wilder Tileston, *Prayers: Ancient and Modern* (New York: Doubleday and McClure, 1897), 80, Internet Archive, https:// archive.org/stream/prayersancienta00tilegoog#page/n92/mode/2up.

6. James L. Mays, *Psalms*, Interpretation: A Bible Commentary for Teaching and Preaching (Louisville, KY: John Knox Press, 1994), 199.

7. Book of Common Prayer (New York: Church Hymnal Corporation, 1979), 355, http://justus.anglican.org/resources/bcp/euchr2.pdf.

THE SECOND WEEK OF LENT

1. Oswald Chambers, *Studies in the Sermon on the Mount* (London: Simpkin Marshall, 1941), 12.

2. Robert A. Guelich, *The Sermon on the Mount: A Foundation for Understanding* (Waco, TX: Word Publishing, 1982), 75.

3. Chambers, *Studies in the Sermon on the Mount*, 12.

4. Roger L. Hahn, *Matthew: A Commentary for Bible Students*, Wesleyan Bible Commentary Series (Indianapolis: Wesleyan Publishing House, 2007), 85.

5. John Bunyan, "The Tenth Stage," in *The Pilgrim's Progress* (Buffalo: Geo. H. Derby and Co., 1853; repr., Christian Classics Ethereal Library), http://www.ccel .org/ccel/bunyan/pilgrim.iv.x.html.

6. Book of Common Prayer, 231, http://justus.anglican.org/resources/bcp /collect_contemp.pdf.

7. Guelich, *Sermon on the Mount*, 82.

8. Manning, *Signature of Jesus*, 74.

9. Thomas More, *The Wisdom and Wit of Blessed Thomas More*, ed. T. E. Bridgett (London: Burns and Oates, 1892), 92-93, Google Books, http://books.google .com/books?id=p2YlAAAAMAAJ&printsec=frontcover&source=gbs_ge_summary_r&cad= 0#v=onepage&q&f=false.

10. Igumen Chariton of Valamo, comp., *The Art of Prayer: An Orthodox Anthology*, trans. E. Kadloubovsky and E. M. Palmer (1966; repr. New York: Faber and Faber, 1997), 149.

11. Dietrich Bonhoeffer, *The Cost of Discipleship* (New York: Macmillan, 1959), 111.

12. Eugene H. Peterson, *Practice Resurrection* (Grand Rapids: Eerdmans Publishing, 2010), 11.

13. Elton Trueblood, *The New Man for Our Time* (New York: Harper and Row, 1970), 66.

14. Prayer by Jeremy Taylor, in Tileston, *Prayers: Ancient and Modern*, 107, Internet Archive, https://archive.org/stream/prayersancienta00tilegoog#page/n118 /mode/2up.

THE THIRD WEEK OF LENT

1. Chambers, *Studies in the Sermon on the Mount*, 16.

2. Book of Common Prayer, 211, http://justus.anglican.org/resources/bcp /collect_contemp.pdf.

3. Chambers, *Studies in the Sermon on the Mount*, 19.

4. Douglas Hare, *Matthew*, Interpretation: A Bible Commentary for Teaching and Preaching (Louisville, KY: John Knox Press, 1993), 45.

5. Prayer from the Sarum Breviary (AD 1085), in Tileston, *Prayers: Ancient and Modern*, 6, Internet Archive, https://archive.org/stream/prayersancienta00tilegoog #page/n18/mode/2up.

6. C. S. Lewis, *Mere Christianity*, rev. ed. (New York: Macmillan Publishing, 1952; repr., New York: HarperCollins, 2001), 92. Citations refer to the HarperCollins edition.

7. Prayer from the Divine Liturgy of the Holy Apostle and Evangelist Mark (before AD 200), in Al Truesdale, ed., *The Book of Saints: The Early Era* (Kansas City: Beacon Hill Press of Kansas City, 2013), 108.

8. Chambers, *Studies in the Sermon on the Mount*, 22.

9. Prayer by Thomas Cranmer, in *For All the Saints*, vol. 1, *Year 1: Advent to the Day of Pentecost*, 844.

10. Chambers, *Studies in the Sermon on the Mount*, 29.

11. Prayer from the Clementine Liturgy (late fourth century), in Truesdale, *Book of Saints*, 17.

12. Book of Common Prayer, 97, http://justus.anglican.org/resources/bcp /mp2.pdf.

13. John Wesley, Sermon 49, "The Cure of Evil-Speaking," in *The Works of John Wesley*, ed. Thomas Jackson, 3rd ed. (London: Wesleyan Methodist Book Room, 1872; repr., Kansas City: Beacon Hill Press of Kansas City, 1986), 6:118.

14. Book of Common Prayer, 255, http://justus.anglican.org/resources/bcp/collect_contemp.pdf.

THE FOURTH WEEK OF LENT

1. MyronS.Augsburger,*Matthew*,TheCommunicator'sCommentary(Waco,TX:Word Books, 1982), 73.

2. Andrew Reed, "Holy Ghost, with Light Divine" (1817), *Hymnary.org*, http://www.hymnary.org/hymn/CBWM1872/257.

3. "The 12 Steps for Freedom from Addictive Behaviors," 12Step.org, http://12step.org/the-12-steps/step-4.htm (accessed December 1, 2014).

4. Chambers, *Studies in the Sermon on the Mount*, 35.

5. John Wesley, a prayer for Friday afternoon from "Devotions for Every Day in the Week," in *A Christian Library* (1750; repr., London: J. Kershaw, 1826), 25:351-52.

6. Alex R. G. Deasley, *Marriage and Divorce in the Bible and the Church* (Kansas City: Beacon Hill Press of Kansas City, 2000), 87.

7. Book of Common Prayer, 179, http://justus.anglican.org/resources/bcp/colctrad.pdf.

8. Guelich, *Sermon on the Mount*, 250.

9. Wesley, *A Collection of Forms of Prayer*, in *Works of John Wesley*, 11:205.

10. Chambers, *Studies in the Sermon on the Mount*, 43.

11. Hahn, *Matthew*, 95.

12. Book of Common Prayer, 816, http://justus.anglican.org/resources/bcp/pray&tnx.pdf.

13. Manning, *Signature of Jesus*, 74.

14. Chambers, *Studies in the Sermon on the Mount*, 52.

15. Prayer by Mary Carpenter, in Tileston, *Prayers: Ancient and Modern*, 43, Internet Archive, https://archive.org/stream/prayersancienta00tilegoog#page/n54/mode/2up.

THE FIFTH WEEK OF LENT

1. Wesley, Sermon 40, "Christian Perfection," in *Works of John Wesley*, 6:1.

2. Attributed to Patrick of Ireland, "I Bind unto Myself Today" (fifth century AD), trans. Cecil F. Alexander (1885), *Hymnary.org*, http://www.hymnary.org/hymn/EH1916/page/735.

3. Mother Teresa of Calcutta, *A Gift for God: Prayers and Meditations* (New York: HarperSanFrancisco, 1996), 52.

4. John Wesley, comments on Matt. 6:8, *Explanatory Notes upon the New Testament* (New York: J. Soule and T. Mason, 1818), 25-26, Google Books, http://books.google.com/books?id=dzI_AAAAYAAJ&printsec=frontcover&source=gbs_ge_summary_r&cad=0#v=onepage&q&f=false.

5. Frederick Buechner, *Whistling in the Dark: A Doubter's Dictionary* (San Francisco: HarperSanFrancisco, 1993), 83-84.

6. George MacDonald, "It Shall Not Be Forgiven," in *Unspoken Sermons Series One* (London: Alexander Strahan, 1867), Christian Classics Ethereal Library (CCEL), http://www.ccel.org/ccel/macdonald/unspoken1.v.html.

7. Book of Common Prayer, 272, http://justus.anglican.org/resources/bcp/Special_Days.pdf.

8. Hannah Whitall Smith, "How to Enter In," chap. 4 in *The Christian's Secret of a Happy Life* (1875), CCEL, http://www.ccel.org/ccel/smith_hw/secret.vi.html.

9. Book of Common Prayer, 219, http://justus.anglican.org/resources/bcp/collect_contemp.pdf.

10. Chambers, *Studies in the Sermon on the Mount*, 67.

11. Adapted from a collect for Ascension Eve, in the Scottish Book of Common Prayer (1929), http://justus.anglican.org/resources/bcp/Scotland/Scot_Easter_Asc_Whit_Readings.htm#Ascension.

THE SIXTH WEEK OF LENT

1. Hahn, *Matthew*, 108.

2. Prayer by James Skinner, in Tileston, *Prayers: Ancient and Modern*, 125, Internet Archive, https://archive.org/stream/prayersancienta00tilegoog#page/n136/mode/2up.

3. Wesley, Sermon 16, "The Means of Grace," in *Works of John Wesley*, 5:190-91.

4. Book of Common Prayer, 208, http://justus.anglican.org/resources/bcp/colctrad.pdf.

5. Chambers, *Studies in the Sermon on the Mount*, 90.

6. Wesley, *A Collection of Forms of Prayer*, in *Works of John Wesley*, 11:205.

7. Evelyn Underhill, *The Spiritual Life* (London: Hodder and Stoughton, 1937; repr., Harrisburg, PA: Morehouse Publishing, 1984), 78.

8. Chambers, *Studies in the Sermon on the Mount*, 104.

9. Prayer from the Sarum Breviary (AD 1085), in Tileston, *Prayers: Ancient and Modern*, 132, Internet Archive, https://archive.org/stream/prayersancienta00tilegoog#page/n144/mode/2up.

10. Wesley, Sermon 33, "Upon Our Lord's Sermon on the Mount: Discourse 13," in *Works of John Wesley*, 5:427.

11. Prayer by Christina G. Rossetti, in Tileston, *Prayers: Ancient and Modern*, 133, Internet Archive, https://archive.org/stream/prayersancienta00tilegoog#page/n144/mode/2up.

12. Hare, *Matthew*, 87.

13. Chambers, *Studies in the Sermon on the Mount*, 110.

14. Prayer from *Book of Prayers* (1851), in Tileston, *Prayers: Ancient and Modern*, 262, Internet Archive, https://archive.org/stream/prayersancienta00tilegoog#page/n274/mode/2up.

HOLY WEEK

1. Book of Common Prayer, 219, http://justus.anglican.org/resources/bcp/collect_contemp.pdf.

2. Ibid., 220.

3. Ibid.

4. Ray Anderson, *The Gospel According to Judas: Is There a Limit to God's Forgiveness?* (Colorado Springs: Helmers and Howard, 1991), 9.

5. Book of Common Prayer, 220, http://justus.anglican.org/resources/bcp/collect_contemp.pdf.

6. Rob L. Staples, *Outward Sign and Inward Grace* (Kansas City: Beacon Hill Press of Kansas City, 1991), 80.

7. Book of Common Prayer, 221, http://justus.anglican.org/resources/bcp/collect_contemp.pdf.

8. *Saving Private Ryan* (1998) Quotes, IMDb, http://www.imdb.com/title/tt0120815/quotes.

9. Ibid.

10. Book of Common Prayer, 221, http://justus.anglican.org/resources/bcp/collect_contemp.pdf.

11. "Were You There?" *Sing to the Lord* (Kansas City: Lillenas Publishing Company, 1993), no. 250.

12. Book of Common Prayer, 221, http://justus.anglican.org/resources/bcp/collect_contemp.pdf.

EASTER DAY

1. Book of Common Prayer, 294, http://justus.anglican.org/resources/bcp/Special_Days.pdf.

2. Ibid., 222, http://justus.anglican.org/resources/bcp/collect_contemp.pdf.

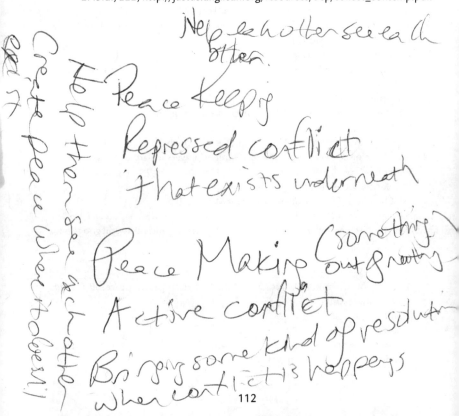